Praise for

Core 52 Student Edition

"*Core 52 Student Edition* provides students with a doable routine for engaging with Scripture and creating long-lasting rhythms for spiritual growth. Both relatable and instructive, Mark has found the balance between digging deep into God's Word and finding its relevance for today."
—MARY SHANNON HOFFPAUIR, Bible teacher, speaker, and author of *Lose Control: The Way to Find Your Soul*

"*Core 52 Student Edition* is perfect for a reader looking to grasp the metanarrative of the Bible in bite-size portions. Parents should use this to help shape their sons and daughters to live like Jesus."
—DUSTIN TAPPAN, director of NextGen at Christ's Church of the Valley, Arizona

"Mark Moore channels his inner Bible professor with *Core 52 Student Edition*. Quick hitting, action packed, biblically accurate, and super relevant—exactly what our youth need in an ever-changing world of what is absolute truth."
—BRIAN BELTRAMO, multiarea director of Fellowship of Christian Athletes, Phoenix, Arizona

"*Core 52 Student Edition* is the recipe that youth culture needs right now! A balanced Bible diet from Mark's book is just the nutrition every Gen Z and millennial should consider for youth-group series, small-group curriculum, and intentional Bible study plans and student leadership development."
—JOHNNY SCOTT, senior pastor of Generations Christian Church, Tampa, Florida

"The challenges and distractions young people face related to spiritual growth are significant. *Core 52 Student Edition* keeps what is most important—learning, memorizing, and applying truth—easy to engage with, relevant, and meaningful."
—ALLY EVANS, NextGen pastor of Life.Church and creator and host of the *LC Parents Podcast*

"As a father of six, I can say there's nothing more important for my kids than deep roots in God's Word. As president of Ozark Christian College where Dr. Moore taught for twenty-two years, I can say there's no one more saturated in Scripture than he. As a student conference speaker for twenty-five years (often with Mark), I can say there's no better biblical communicator to young people than Mark Moore. As his friend, I can say there's no one who's genuinely seeking to live for the God of the Word more than Mark."

—MATT PROCTOR, president of Ozark Christian College,
Joplin, Missouri

"Somehow, God packed a deep theologian, a passionate and powerful disciple maker, and one of the most articulate communicators I've ever met into one man: Mark Moore."

—MATT REAGAN, associate pastor of Southeast Christian Church,
Louisville, Kentucky

"Mark Moore has written a discipleship resource for students that truly respects their desire to go beyond the surface. Rather than writing trite devotionals, Mark has thoughtfully explored questions that Christ-following young people are asking or ought to be asking. The search for identity is so critical, and *Core 52 Student Edition* wastes no time digging into topics such as who am I, who Jesus is, and what difference knowing his mission will have for my life."

—KEVIN GREER, professor of student ministries at Ozark Christian
College, Joplin, Missouri

"Mark Moore is a Bible teacher, a motivator, a coach, a teacher, and an all-around leadership guru! If you have teenagers in your ministry or living under your roof who want to read the Bible on their own but have never quite gotten in the habit, put this book in their hands!"

—KURT JOHNSTON, NextGen pastor of Saddleback Church,
Lake Forest, California

CORE
52
Student Edition

CORE

Student Edition

A FIFTEEN-MINUTE DAILY GUIDE
TO BUILD YOUR BIBLE IQ IN A YEAR

MARK E. MOORE

WATERBROOK

Published in the United States by WaterBrook, an imprint of Random House,
a division of Penguin Random House LLC.

WATERBROOK® and its deer colophon are registered trademarks
of Penguin Random House LLC.

LIBRARY OF CONGRESS CATALOGING-IN-PUBLICATION DATA
Names: Moore, Mark E. (Mark Edward), 1963— author.
Title: Core 52 student edition : a fifteen-minute daily guide to build your Bible IQ
in a year / Mark E. Moore.
Other titles: Core fifty-two student edition
Description: First edition. | Colorado Springs : WaterBrook, 2021.
Identifiers: LCCN 2020013717 | ISBN 9780593193556 (trade paperback) |
ISBN 9780593193563 (ebook)
Subjects: LCSH: Bible—Textbooks. | Christian teenagers—Religious life.
Classification: LCC BS605.3 .M662 2021 | DDC 220.3—dc23
LC record available at https://lccn.loc.gov/2020013717

Printed in the United States of America on acid-free paper

waterbrookmultnomah.com

2 4 6 8 9 7 5 3 1

First Edition

Interior book design by Virginia Norey

SPECIAL SALES
Most WaterBrook books are available at special quantity discounts
when purchased in bulk by corporations, organizations, and special-interest groups.
Custom imprinting or excerpting can also be done to fit special needs. For information,
please email specialmarketscms@penguinrandomhouse.com.

To Larrie Fraley and Jason Beck

* * *

Though a man might prevail against one who is alone, two will withstand him—a threefold cord is not quickly broken.

—ECCLESIASTES 4:12

Contents

Introduction

From Curiosity to Confidence

If you're like most Christ followers, you want to know the Bible better. You keep hearing pastors and parents talk about its importance. But can we be honest? For many students the Bible seems boring or even irrelevant. Yet something in you knows that it matters to you. How else are you going to discover and live out God's purpose for you?

And then there's this little fact: the Bible is only the most influential piece of literature in all human history.

There's a good reason for that fact. Knowing the Bible better makes us better at life. It's true. People who read the Bible four times a week or more reduce loneliness by 30 percent and self-destructive thoughts by 32 percent and increase their ability to forgive by 31 percent.[1] That's huge! But realistically, how can you read and understand this big old book called the Bible?

Core 52 Student Edition offers a clear plan that can actually fit into your crazy schedule. If you can carve out fifteen minutes a day, five days a week, for one year, you can move from curiosity about God's Word to confidence in it. That sounds like a pretty bold claim, but this goal is well within reach. You hold in your hands an encounter with fifty-two of the most powerful passages for Christians—kind of a SparkNotes to the Bible. By grasping these "vital few" verses, you'll wrap your mind around the entire Bible with minimal time and effort.

Let me introduce myself. For twenty-two years, I was a New Testament professor at Ozark Christian College. My job was to train pastors. In 2012, I traded my Professor Moore title for that of Pastor Mark at Christ's Church of the Valley in Phoenix. It's one of those ridiculously large churches that are often more comfortable for those who've never been to church than for those who grew up in church. I serve as a teaching pastor, helping navigate that intimidating book called the Bible.

Core 52 Student Edition brings to the surface the freshest water from the deepest well. People's buckets hold only so much, so I've chosen core passages with the highest impact. With this core, you can go further faster toward confidence in God and your own spiritual experience. Think of me as your personal trainer for spiritual growth. With the help of the Holy Spirit, you'll make the most of your strategic investment in Scripture. And you'll exponentially increase both your personal growth and your impact on our world.

So, here's the plan:

- **Day 1:** *Read the essay.* Following the essay are three key points to check for comprehension. If any of them are unclear, reread those portions of the essay. (You may find it helpful to read the key points before reading the essay so you know what to look for.) You can also watch a brief teaching video each week at www.core52.org or find the Core52 playlist on YouTube.
- **Day 2:** *Memorize the core text,* and review verses from the previous two weeks.
- **Day 3:** *Read a story or other passage from the Bible* that illustrates the text of the week. By reading these stories in light of the core text, you'll notice how key principles were expressed in the real lives of God's people.

- **Day 4:** *Read through the three trajectory passages,* meditating on their implications and connections. You might begin by reviewing the core text from memory.
- **Day 5:** *Put key principles into practice* by scheduling a time for the action step. Most exercises should take no more than thirty minutes, and each should be accomplished that week. That's the best way to embed a new principle in practical application.

Welcome to the journey from curiosity to confidence. You can do this! By mastering the core of God's Word, you'll build a firm framework for becoming a Christ-centered difference maker in your own circle of influence.

God has designed you uniquely for such a time as this. You're needed more now than ever.

Why Am I Here?

In the beginning, God created the heavens and the earth.

—Genesis 1:1

You and I are hurtling through an immense universe on a little blue ball called planet Earth. It's only natural to wonder, *Why am I here?*

You might think I'd have this figured out by now. I'm a father of two, a grandfather of eight, a pastor, and a professor with decades of life experience. Yet there are still days when I wrestle with the question. Maybe you can relate.

All I can tell you is that the best answer I've ever found is at the beginning of the Bible. And it starts not with *Why* but with *Who.*

Who Created This World?

We learn from the opening sentences of the Bible what our Creator is like (Genesis 1:1–3). All artists leave fingerprints. Their creations reveal their character. The same is true for God.

God the Father is the architect. Not only did he create the earth, but he also made matter itself. And that matters. You see, every other ancient religion thought matter was eternal and the gods merely shaped it into the world we know. It's basically the same idea as Darwinian evolution—matter has always somehow existed. The Bible says something different. It credits the one true God for both the shape of the world and the stuff it's made from.

The Holy Spirit is the engineer. As we read in verse 2, "The earth was without form and void, and darkness was over the face of the deep. And the Spirit of God was hovering over the face of the waters." The Hebrew word for "hovering" describes a vibration. The Spirit "quaked" to bring order out of chaos. It's kind of like your mother thirty minutes before dinner guests arrive.

More than that, the Spirit breathed life into Adam (2:7) just as he does for you. With every breath you take, the Spirit is coursing through you. (This is also true of animals, according to Psalm 104:30.) The Spirit is relentlessly, intimately, and perpetually involved in the fabric of our world.

When people ignore the Spirit's role in creation, the environment becomes a resource to be exploited rather than a gift to be nurtured. We miss the Spirit in the wind, the bloom of a flower, and the majesty of the mountains. Consequently, Christians often limit worship to a building on Sunday, rather than worshipping daily in the expanse of the universe. God the Father *created;* God the Spirit *creates.*

Jesus is the builder. He did the heavy lifting during the Creation. This fact is seen in Genesis 1:3: "God said, 'Let there be light,' and there was light." Fast-forward to John 1:1–3: "In the beginning was the Word, and the Word was with God, and the Word was God. He was in the beginning with God. All things were made through him, and without him was not any thing made that was made." This Word is none other than Jesus (verse 14). Before Jesus came to earth, he created the earth. When God gave the command, Jesus—the Word—turned the command into creation.

The apostle Paul described it this way:

He is the image of the invisible God, the firstborn of all creation. For by him all things were created, in heaven and on earth, visible and invisible, whether thrones or dominions or rulers or authorities—all things were created through him and for him. (Colossians 1:15–16)

When we ignore the role of Jesus in creation, we focus on getting to heaven rather than bringing heaven to earth through social justice: care for people and their environment. Jesus cares about what happens on the earth he created!

So, there you have it: God is the architect, the Holy Spirit is the engineer, and Jesus is the builder. If we ignore any of these truths, we'll misunderstand not only the nature of creation but also our own nature and God's purpose for us here on earth.

Which gets us to *Why*.

Why Did God Create This World?

Psalm 102:18 provides the answer: "Let this be recorded for a generation to come, so that a people yet to be created may praise the LORD." God created so his creation would bring him glory. We do the same thing. We dress to impress. We flaunt our swag. We perform on stage and on the field to please others and receive praise. God creates with the same impulse. He wants us to recognize and enjoy what he made for us.

Why not? What he made is praiseworthy, and it starts with our own bodies. Our fingerprints, the structure of our eyes, the electrical synapses of our brains—our bodies are works of art. From Olympic spectacles to ballet, from the NBA to National Geographic, we're stunned by God's handiwork. David expressed it well: "You formed my inward parts; you knitted me together in my mother's womb" (139:13). God's fingerprints are all over us!

And God made us to manage his creation: "We are his workmanship, created in Christ Jesus for good works, which God prepared beforehand, that we should walk in them" (Ephesians 2:10). We partner with God to carry on creation. God created the heavens and the earth—he leaves it up to us to make a world that's wonderful.

In many ways, we have. Think about human achievements in art, science, literature, music, athletics. In other ways, we've failed miserably! All around, we see the consequences of human brokenness. Yet the last chapter of human history has yet to be written, although the end, of course, has begun in the story of Jesus: "If anyone is in Christ, he is a new creation. The old has passed away; behold, the new has come" (2 Corinthians 5:17). There's not a quick fix or an easy solution. But someday we will see the beautiful restoration of Eden, and you can be part of that:

> The creation waits with eager longing for the revealing of the sons of God. . . . We know that the whole creation has been groaning together in the pains of childbirth until now. (Romans 8:19, 22)

Key Points

- The Father, Son, and Spirit each play a vital role in creation.

- God created for the same reasons we do: for others' pleasure and our own praise.

- Just as God *created* the earth, we're to continue to *re-create* a world reflecting his love.

This Week

☐ **Day 1:** Read the essay. Then note in the margins something you learned about yourself.

☐ **Day 2:** Memorize Genesis 1:1.

☐ **Day 3:** Read Genesis 1–2. What does the record of our beginnings reveal about your life's purpose?

☐ **Day 4:** Write down the question "Why am I here?" Then see what answers you find in John 1:1–3, Ephesians 2:10, and Colossians 1:15–16.

☐ **Day 5:** In what ways are you creative or talented? Art, music, poetry, encouragement, food, something else? Create something to give to someone, joining God in making a beautiful world.

Who Am I?

God said, "Let us make man in our image."

—GENESIS 1:26

As a middle child, I remember feeling a bit overlooked. Like I didn't matter. Maybe wasn't even there. Nobody wants to feel that way! We want to know that we're noticed and that we matter.

What if I told you that God takes a special interest in *you*? That *you* are his pride and joy? Well, that's the truth!

> God said, "Let us make man in our image, after our likeness. And let them have dominion over the fish of the sea and over the birds of the heavens and over the livestock and over all the earth and over every creeping thing that creeps on the earth."
>
> So God created man in his own image,
>   in the image of God he created him;
>   male and female he created them. (Genesis 1:26–27)

You and I are created in God's own image. In his likeness. That does not mean humans are the same as God, but we do share many of his qualities. This simple observation can change everything. So, let's jump into this week's core verse and discover who we really are.

The Power of "Us"

God said, "Let *us* make man in our image" (verse 26). Notice God is three in one: Father, Son, and Spirit. This is a mystery we'll never fully understand, but we, like God, experience community every day. You see, God created us *in* community and *for* community.

Our culture makes this truth difficult to accept. Our words reflect our radical individualism: "You do you!" "You gotta find what's right for you." "Who are you to tell me how to live?" This kind of individualism will leave us feeling lost and empty.

Even our language in church focuses on individuality. Consider these examples:

1. Jesus is called our *personal* Lord and Savior.
2. Bible reading is part of our *personal* devotions, even though the majority of the books in the Bible were written to communities, not individuals.
3. We think of prayer as primarily private. In Bible times, it was far more public (1 Timothy 2:8).

Radical individualism denies our true identity. We are part of something greater. God made us to reflect him by living *in* community and *for* community. In fact, your character and mine are nearly always forged in community.

In His Own Image

A second big idea from this week's core passage is God's *image*. But what does that mean? God is spirit, not flesh. So, how do we share his image?

Animals, humans, and God all share certain emotions: joy, affection, sorrow, compassion, and so forth. Animals and humans share a number of attributes, such as bodies that have cravings and the ability to feel shame. So, there are some attributes only animals and humans share and some they share with God. Our divine character, however, lies in those attributes we share with God.

The image of God in humans makes us care about honor, time, beauty, language, love, and rule. Let's take a closer look.

Honor is the underlying driver for almost everything we do. It's why we dress up, work out, and brush our teeth. We *need* (I don't use this word lightly) to be honored. When this God-given desire goes bad, it's called pride and always results in idolatry.

Our awareness of *time*. Though he's eternal, God works *in* time. He knows the past and has his eye on the future. Therefore, when we plan parties, look at our watches, or count down till Christmas, we're exercising the divine nature in us.

Beauty! We're the only creatures that make art, post to Instagram, or dress up for prom. Not only do we create beauty, but we also *constantly* create it. New music releases weekly. Our favorite video games add new levels. Netflix, YouTube, and Disney+ exist! Since the beginning of time, humans have constantly created beauty. Why? Because we can't help exercising God's nature in us.

Language is uniquely human. From poetry to rap, mathematics to inside jokes, we use language. A child can speak to an imaginary friend! We tweet, text, and post. Our need for communication is a direct reflection of the divine spark in us.

Then there's *love*. Now, you might argue that animals love, and you wouldn't be wrong. Animals protect their young. Pets bond with people. But no animal would sacrifice its life for someone it has never met. No animal has ever given sacrificially to victims of an earthquake. The noblest feature God gave us is our capacity to love another simply because he or she is a person.

Finally, God created us to *rule*. King David composed a song about this fact:

You have made him a little lower than the heavenly beings
    and crowned him with glory and honor.
You have given him dominion over the works of your hands;
    you have put all things under his feet. . . .

O Lord, our Lord,
    how majestic is your name in all the earth! (Psalm 8:5–6, 9)

We're caretakers of God's garden. Our purpose is to enhance what God made. Each of us has abilities to do so. Our every creative act, whether musical, architectural, athletic, or intellectual, is a partnership with God.

When we're ruled by the earth rather than being rulers of it, we fail as God's agents. When we give in to lust, greed, fear, and violence, the result is addiction, poverty, pain, and alienation. Through Jesus, the perfect man, God gave us a second chance to live up to our purpose (Hebrews 2:6–8).

Made for a Purpose

So, worship God as David did: "I praise you, for I am fearfully and wonderfully made. Wonderful are your works; my soul knows it very well" (Psalm 139:14). We were made *for a purpose* by God. And we were made for an incredible purpose—to care for others and the earth in partnership with God. That's our identity, which Jesus restored to us by becoming one of us.

Key Points

- Our true identity is found in community, not in individualism.
- God's divine nature in us is exercised in the simplest acts of conversation, art, planning, shared meals, etc.
- Our divine design enables and requires us to participate with God in the ongoing act of creation.

This Week

☐ **Day 1:** After reading the essay, jot down in the margin a few characteristics you have that reflect God in you.

☐ **Day 2:** Memorize Genesis 1:26.

☐ **Day 3:** Read Ephesians 1. What does it tell you about who you are that the Genesis story doesn't?

☐ **Day 4:** What do you learn about your identity from Psalm 8:5–6, Psalm 139:13–14, and Hebrews 2:6–8?

☐ **Day 5:** We claim an important part of our true identity when we take community seriously. Pick three friends and think about what abilities and characteristics they have that reflect God's nature. (Your friends don't need to be Christians, just humans.) Then share what you see with them. It will blow their minds.

What Is My Problem?

When the woman saw that the tree was good for food, and that
it was a delight to the eyes, and that the tree was to be desired
to make one wise, she took of its fruit and ate, and she also gave
some to her husband who was with her, and he ate.

—GENESIS 3:6

I remember my visit to Auschwitz, the notorious Nazi concentration camp. I walked in thinking, *How could they?* But along with everyone else in our group, I walked out in stunned silence. Later, I pulled out my journal and wrote these chilling words: "After today, I can relate to the German soldiers." They were just people like me.

In my more honest moments, I see my capacity to reject God and hurt other people. Badly. Sooner or later, we find that we are capable of more evil than we ever imagined.

It all started in a garden.

The story is told in Genesis 3. It begins with a careless woman, a checked-out husband, a talking snake, and forbidden fruit. Eve knew the fruit was off limits. Yet Satan tricked her. She took the bait in a bite while Adam stood by, silent. But afterward, Eve's eyes were opened. She had lost her innocence. Adam had too. Can you relate?

Adam and Eve's failure isn't foreign. They represent all of us—adult, teen, male, female. We've all experienced temptation, taken the bait, and suffered the consequences.

Obviously, every human at some point asks, *What is my problem?*

Irresistible Temptation

First, notice what captured Eve's attention, because it's the same thing that captures ours. It was Satan's promise "You will be like God" (verse 5). The prideful idea that we control our own lives.

Pride isn't merely *a* sin; it's *the* sin. Look behind every murder, theft, lie, and addiction. That's why the Bible warns against pride so often: "Pride goes before destruction, and a haughty spirit before a fall" (Proverbs 16:18). "Whoever exalts himself will be humbled, and whoever humbles himself will be exalted" (Matthew 23:12). "God opposes the proud but gives grace to the humble" (James 4:6; 1 Peter 5:5; paraphrasing Proverbs 3:34). Pride is a subplot of nearly every book of the Bible because it's the source of our broken human condition.

Then again, we probably don't need to read about it in a book. We see it in the mirror.

Society praises pride and independence, even though they are killing us as individuals and as a culture. That's why it's so important that we lay down pride and imitate Jesus by serving others. Self-improvement, self-respect, and self-management are all good, but they can never rescue us from the grip of sin. Why? Because we're still relying on ourselves.

Eve's story was summarized thousands of years later by Jesus's best friend, John:

> Do not love the world or the things in the world. If anyone loves the
> world, the love of the Father is not in him. For all that is in the
> world—the desires of the flesh and the desires of the eyes and pride of
> life—is not from the Father but is from the world. (1 John 2:15–16)

Deadly Deception

Satan lied to Eve. He said she wouldn't die if she ate the forbidden fruit (Genesis 3:4). Did she die?

Technically, no—at least, not at that moment. Would she die? Absolutely. We all do—because our choices are just like Eve's. However, Satan's deception is not a bold-faced lie. It's half-true. Satan promises it'll feel good, give you a buzz, or satisfy a craving. He's not wrong! But the future pain far outweighs the momentary pleasure. There is always a price tag for cheating, viewing pornography, partying, or stealing. But Satan keeps that part secret. Besides, most of the time, we're pretty sure we can beat the odds. (There's that pride thing again.)

Like Eve, we focus on the promise of delight. But one surrender to temptation and we're stuck with the consequences, sometimes for a long time. This no-win situation is the curse of sin. The cost of sin is as high as our God is holy.

God's Reckoning

God cursed Adam and Eve because they were guilty of rebellion. Taking the fruit wasn't merely theft; it was mutiny—an attempt to become like God. Eve rejected God himself. She had (and we have) the audacity to challenge God's eternal wisdom, his perfect plan, and his moral authority.

When you think about it, that's outrageous! Are you God? Am I? The truth is, no human has the power to manage his or her own life without God's direction. But people try all the time. How many people's lives have spiraled out of control under the weight of their own arrogance?

Adam and Eve were kicked out of the garden, but—get this—it was *for their own good* (Genesis 3:22–24). How is exile good? Because the garden is not our goal; the heart of God is. It's useless to live in luxury if you lose your character and your connection to your Creator.

If you have sensed a void in your life, what you're really missing is connection to your Creator. The curse calls us back to our original relationship. We return to God through repentance, retracing our steps to submission to our Creator.

Here's the good news. First, our Creator sent his own son, Jesus, to pay the price to remove the curse of sin. Second, the Son of God sent his Holy Spirit to support us so we could do better than Adam and Eve. And we have God's promise on that: "No temptation has overtaken you that is not common to man. God is faithful, and he will not let you be tempted beyond your ability, but with the temptation he will also provide the way of escape, that you may be able to endure it" (1 Corinthians 10:13).

Key Points

- Pride says, "It's all about me." That's why pride is the root of every sin.

- Sin tempts with half truths, not blatant lies.

- From the first fall, God had a rescue plan. He sent his own son to bring us back to him.

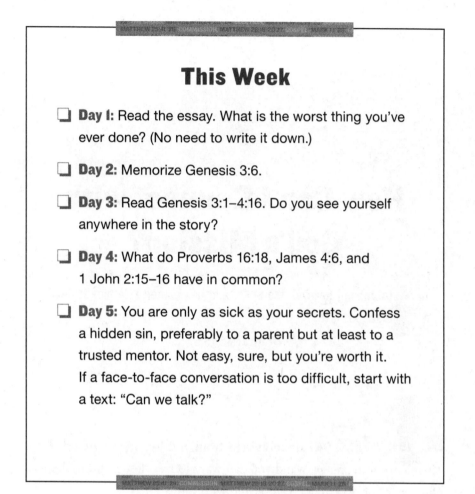

This Week

☐ **Day I:** Read the essay. What is the worst thing you've ever done? (No need to write it down.)

☐ **Day 2:** Memorize Genesis 3:6.

☐ **Day 3:** Read Genesis 3:1–4:16. Do you see yourself anywhere in the story?

☐ **Day 4:** What do Proverbs 16:18, James 4:6, and 1 John 2:15–16 have in common?

☐ **Day 5:** You are only as sick as your secrets. Confess a hidden sin, preferably to a parent but at least to a trusted mentor. Not easy, sure, but you're worth it. If a face-to-face conversation is too difficult, start with a text: "Can we talk?"

4

How Can I Connect with God's Mission?

> [Abraham] believed the LORD, and he counted it to him as righteousness.
>
> —GENESIS 15:6

Do you ever feel disconnected from and forgotten by God? I do. There's not some magic wand you can wave to feel close to him. There is, however, a way to build a relationship with him.

That's what Abraham's story is all about. Most of us don't realize that more people follow Abraham than Jesus. By far! He is considered the father of the faith by Jews, Muslims, *and* Christians. That is 55 percent of the entire planet!

As this week's verse says, "He believed the LORD, and *he counted it to him as righteousness.*" The New Testament repeats this line about Abraham several times (Romans 4; Galatians 3:6; James 2:23).

God called Abraham to leave his family and his land in ancient Iraq. Abraham obeyed with little to go on. By the time he was eighty-five, he didn't have any children or a single square foot of land. Even so, Abraham never gave up on God, and eventually God fulfilled every promise he had ever made to Abraham.

That fact is important because we stand at the receiving end of those promises when we put our faith in Jesus. The Bible word for this kind of promise is *covenant* (or *testament*).

A covenant is basically an agreement between two parties. The rules were simple: (1) the more important of the two parties established the conditions; (2) these conditions spelled out the rewards for keeping the contract and the punishment for breaking it; and (3) the covenant was typically "signed" by a blood sacrifice. That's how serious it was. The person accepting the agreement would cut an animal in half (gruesome, I know). Then he would walk between the two halves of the sacrifice as if to say, "If I break this agreement, may it be to me as I have done to this animal." So, a bit more significant than a handshake.

That's exactly what God did with Abraham in Genesis 15:7–21, only it was God, not Abraham, who walked between the sacrifice, saying, "If *you* break this covenant, I will pay the price." That's crazy! And that's exactly what Jesus did for us.

Abraham's Covenant Fulfilled in Jesus

Aside from Abraham's, the two most important covenants in the Bible make up the Old and New Testaments. The first came through Moses (the law); the second, through Jesus (grace). With this distinction in mind, let's look specifically at Abraham's covenant. Doing so will help us understand our own covenant in Christ. God made this promise to Abraham:

> I will make of you a great nation, and I will bless you and make your name great, so that you will be a blessing. I will bless those who bless you, and him who dishonors you I will curse, and in you all the families of the earth shall be blessed. (12:2–3)

Look again at the last sentence. It guaranteed that Abraham's offspring would have a global impact. The question is, How? Most rabbis understood the promise to mean that people who came to Israel, adopted her customs, and changed their ways would be blessed because of their conversion. Come to Israel, become Israel, and you'll be blessed with Israel.

However, there were some rabbis—Jesus included—who understood the promise of Abraham to be outward focused. Outsiders don't come to us, but we are to go to them. The earth would be blessed because we leave our homes to go where God leads and to say what God says. This act of taking God's love to the world would result in the inclusion of all cultures, not the protection of a single culture. The best Old Testament example of this is Jonah. The prophet Jonah wanted to be inward focused; God sent him on a mission outside Israel.

Big picture: When we keep God's covenant God's way, good things tend to come our way. When we try to make God do things our way, well, let me tell you—it doesn't work!

Why Does All This Matter?

As a student trying to follow Jesus, this affects you in two ways.

First, *you're in a covenantal relationship with God.* This reality implies both responsibility and community. God invites us into something bigger than ourselves. We call it the church, but it's bigger than that. It's a kingdom! This kingdom goes back to our father Abraham, whom we follow as an example of faith.

There's more "we" than "me" in following Jesus. When we lose sight of the covenant, we focus on keeping rules rather than building relationships. Our focus should be on living on mission in the community in order to take God's love to a broken world.

Second, *Jesus fulfills the major covenants.*

- Abraham was asked to sacrifice his promised son, Isaac. At the last second, an angel intervened and God provided a ram, so

Abraham named the place "The LORD will provide" (Genesis 22:14). This event pointed forward to Jesus, the lamb whom God provided.

- The night before Jesus died, he connected the covenant of Moses (the law) with the new covenant of grace. The Passover[1] lamb foreshadowed[2] "the Lamb of God, who takes away the sin of the world" (John 1:29). Matthew 26:27–28 memorializes the moment: "He took a cup, and when he had given thanks he gave it to them, saying, 'Drink of it, all of you, for this is *my blood of the covenant,* which is poured out for many for the forgiveness of sins.'"

Key Points

- Abraham's trust (faith) in God is the model of faithfulness for Christians today.

- A covenant is an agreement between two parties that includes conditions, terms, and consequences.

- Jesus paved a way for us to have an authentic relationship with God.

This Week

❑ **Day 1:** After reading the essay, write down five things or people you trust in. (Money? Boyfriend/girlfriend? Popularity? Technology? Science?) Be as honest as you can. Number them in the order that you trust most.

❑ **Day 2:** Memorize Genesis 15:6.

❑ **Day 3:** Read Genesis 21:1–7 and 22:1–18. How do you think you would have responded if you were Abraham, Sarah, Isaac?

❑ **Day 4:** Read Genesis 12:1–9, Romans 4, and Galatians 3:6. Jot down some lessons you could learn from Abraham.

❑ **Day 5:** Come up with a practical way to show God's love to a hurting person this week.

How Do I Get Right with God?

I am the LORD who brought you up out of the land of Egypt to be your God. You shall therefore be holy, for I am holy.

—LEVITICUS 11:45

Holy. **The word sounds** so heavy. Unappealing. *Impossible,* really. It makes me think of priests and incense, cathedrals and boring sermons. Oh, and it leaves me feeling . . . guilty.

Ugh.

Am I a bad person for admitting this? Well, it's true. That's why I was so encouraged to learn that the word *holy* doesn't really mean "sacred" as much as "selected." This subtle distinction makes a big difference in how we view ourselves, church, *and* God.

The Proclamation of Holiness

What makes something holy? Holiness happens when God takes ordinary objects and claims them for himself. For example, an ordinary plot of ground becomes sacred if God shows up. An ordinary animal, set aside for sacrifice, suddenly becomes consecrated.[1] A person elected by God becomes a priest or a prophet. These become sacred not because their nature is changed but because their purpose is changed. In one moment, they were ordinary. In the next, God claims them as his own.

Holiness happens when God proclaims us holy, not when we perform holy acts. Holiness is received, not achieved. Is holiness also something we practice? Well, of course it is. However, our practice of holiness is the *result* of God's proclamation of holiness, not the other way around.

Here's an example. A toothbrush is an ordinary object that has dozens of potential uses. Yet once you put it in your mouth, it's *yours* and you don't want anyone else using it for anything else. Why (aside from the fact that it's gross)? Because when ordinary objects are used for special service, they become out of bounds, or—to use a Bible word—holy.

Let me restate the big idea here before we move on. *You are holy not because of your performance but because of God's proclamation.* You don't become holy through religious ritual. You don't develop holiness through sheer discipline. You become holy the millisecond God places his hand on you and says, "Mine."

With that truth in mind, let's look at this chapter's key verse. In Leviticus 11:45, God said, "I am the LORD who brought you up out of the land of Egypt to be your God. You shall therefore be holy, for I am holy."

Of all the nations on earth, God placed his hand on Israel and said, "Mine." From that moment on, Israel was holy. As Exodus 19:6 says, "You shall be to me a kingdom of priests and a holy nation." Were they always holy in behavior? Not so much. But they did belong to God.

God always intended for his followers to have both personal access to him and a sacred purpose. In the New Testament, after Jesus's death and resurrection, one of his key leaders, the apostle Peter, repeated the decree from Exodus—only this time he applied it to the church: "You are a chosen race, a royal priesthood, a holy nation, a people for his own possession, that you may proclaim the excellencies of him who called you out of darkness into his marvelous light" (1 Peter 2:9). That's talking about *you.* You belong to God, and he has a purpose for your life.

The Practice of Holiness

Holiness happens when God shows up. It's first his presence and then his proclamation that make us holy. Afterward, we should live up to what he says about us—that we are his children who reflect his good name.

What does this kind of holiness look like? Here's an example:

Jake was a naturally likable kid. He was a blast to hang out with. Unfortunately, his father wasn't around. This didn't make Jake bitter, just unwise. So throughout high school he always opted for the shortest route to immediate pleasure. Because he was the life of the party, he preferred the party life. As one might expect, sports, girls, and drugs all came easily, which doesn't make life easy. Jake spent most of his high school days in a low-grade buzz that became a raging rave on the weekends.

Then he met Jesus. After graduation, his former high school soccer coach invited him to church. He heard the simple message of the gospel with a clear head. Jake decided to follow Jesus. He was immediately marked and eternally sanctified.[2] As Jake's circle of friends changed, so did his pleasures and pastimes. This isn't one of those crazy grace stories with a miraculous intervention. It's simply the normal process of meeting someone who wins your allegiance. For Jake, giving up partying, drugs, and drinking was not a hard-fought struggle. It was like pushing aside a salad when the steak comes to the table.

But holiness can be challenging. We have to make tough choices. Sex now or a strong marriage later? Cheat to boost my grade, or keep my character but risk losing a scholarship? Usually we know what's right. When we wrestle with holiness, it's not because we really believe that the world has a better offer. It's usually because we forget one of two realities: God is with us. And God has declared us holy.

In our culture, holy living sounds old fashioned, even stifling. However, think in terms of eternity. Sacrifice now means unimaginable rewards later. And even in the here and now, God's ways are truly better. They lead to the greatest happiness a person can experience on earth.

And when you think about it, doesn't God's election of us deserve our best representation of him?

Key Points

- Holiness is in your election more than in your action.

- Israel was called to be a kingdom of priests. The church fulfilled that calling.

- Righteous behavior is the appropriate and natural response for everyone who is called to live out God's purpose.

This Week

☐ **Day 1:** After reading the essay, how might your list of holy things change?

☐ **Day 2:** Memorize Leviticus 11:45.

☐ **Day 3:** How can someone who sins still be holy? Look for the answer in 2 Samuel 11 and Psalm 51.

☐ **Day 4:** If someone asked you what holiness is, which of these verses—Exodus 19:6, 2 Corinthians 7:1, or 1 Peter 2:9—would you use to help explain it?

☐ **Day 5:** You are a child of God. That's your God-given identity. Write down one thing you must *stop* and one you must *start* to be who you truly are.

6

Is Jesus as Good as They Say?

> I will raise up for them a prophet like you from among their brothers. And I will put my words in his mouth, and he shall speak to them all that I command him.
>
> —DEUTERONOMY 18:18

Who is the GOAT? LeBron James or Michael Jordan? Tiger Woods or Jack Nicklaus? Tom Brady or Joe Montana? Debating who is the greatest of all time is fun in sports but gets nasty in politics. Can you imagine any modern president claiming, "I am greater than George Washington"? Well, that's pretty much what Jesus did. Moses was the founder of their nation, the liberator of the Jews, and the one who gave Israel the Ten Commandments. Yet Jesus had the audacity to claim to be greater than Moses. The astounding thing is that virtually every writer of the New Testament agreed!

We can start with Jesus himself. In the Sermon on the Mount, six times he said something like "Moses said . . . but I say" (Matthew 5:17–48). Pretty gutsy, given the religious climate. Jesus clearly saw himself not merely as an authoritative interpreter of the law of Moses but as one who could fulfill and even extend it.

Matthew seems to have shaped his entire book in the shadow of Moses. Both Jesus and Moses were tested in the desert. Both were known as humble leaders (Numbers 12:3; Matthew 11:29; 21:5). Moses and Jesus had a conversation on top of a mountain during the Transfiguration (17:3).[1] Finally, Jesus's Last Supper was during the Passover meal that Moses established (26:17–29). Clearly Moses foreshadowed Jesus.

John was another eyewitness to Jesus's life. He recorded Jesus saying he was like Moses's serpent on a staff, which healed people of their sins (Numbers 21:4–9). Anyone who looked at the raised serpent by faith was healed of the snakebite. Jesus compared his crucifixion to the bronze serpent of Moses: "As Moses lifted up the serpent in the wilderness, so must the Son of Man be lifted up, that whoever believes in him may have eternal life" (John 3:14–15).

A few chapters later, there's a discussion about manna, bread given miraculously by God (6:26–58). Jesus said, "Truly, truly, I say to you, it was not Moses who gave you the bread from heaven, but my Father gives you the true bread from heaven. For the bread of God is he who comes down from heaven and gives life to the world" (verses 32–33). The Israelites under Moses ate manna and died, but Jesus is the bread from heaven that provides eternal life (verses 48–51).

The apostle Paul also connected Jesus and Moses. In 1 Corinthians 10:1–4, Jesus isn't compared to Moses the liberator. Rather, Jesus is the rock from which the Israelites drank: "All drank the same spiritual drink. For they drank from the spiritual Rock that followed them, and the Rock was Christ" (verse 4; see also Exodus 17:6). In other words, Moses was God's messenger to Israel, but Jesus was God's gift to Israel.

In 2 Corinthians 3:13–18, Paul recalled an incident in Exodus 34:33. After Moses met with God on Mount Sinai, his face literally shone because of being in the presence of God, but the light did not last long. To hide the fading glory, Moses veiled his face after speaking to the crowd.

When Paul compared Moses with Jesus, he contrasted the fading glory of Moses with the unfading glory of Jesus on the Christian: "We all, with unveiled face, beholding the glory of the Lord, are being transformed into the same image from one degree of glory to another. For this comes from the Lord who is the Spirit" (2 Corinthians 3:18).

In summary, Jesus is not Moses. Or the New Testament version of Moses. He's better! Moses was God's messenger. Jesus is the very means by which we connect with God.

This is precisely the point of Hebrews 3:3–6:

> Jesus has been counted worthy of more glory than Moses—as much more glory as the builder of a house has more honor than the house itself. (For every house is built by someone, but the builder of all things is God.) Now Moses was faithful in all God's house as a servant, to testify to the things that were to be spoken later, but Christ is faithful over God's house as a son. And we are his house, if indeed we hold fast our confidence and our boasting in our hope.

Nearly every author of the New Testament suggested that Jesus is superior to Moses. Moses instituted the Passover; Jesus is the Passover lamb. Moses offered manna; Jesus is the bread from heaven. Moses miraculously provided water from the rock; Jesus is that rock.

Most of us today don't think much about whether Jesus is greater than Moses. But we face the same question in other ways. Is Jesus greater than Buddha or Muhammad? Greater than any other spiritual path, no matter how popular or appealing? If so, is surrendering our lives to Jesus Christ a good answer to our deepest need, or is it the *only* answer?

Two things place Jesus in a category all his own. First, his incomparable moral life demonstrated the power of God on human soil. Second, he rose from the dead, proving he is God's son. Without Jesus's life, death, and resurrection, there's no way he could claim to have fulfilled the prophecy about Moses, let alone surpassed his status.

Which brings us to the real question: What are you going to do about it? If Jesus is as good as they say, ignoring him is *not* an option.

Key Points

- In Jesus's day, any claim that Jesus is greater than Moses would have raised more than eyebrows. It would have raised religious rage.

- Nearly every author of the New Testament claimed that Jesus is better than Moses.

- Any explanation of Jesus's superiority to Moses must be grounded in Jesus's flawless moral life and in his resurrection. We dare not ignore him.

This Week

☐ **Day 1:** Read the essay. What other important leaders is Jesus superior to?

☐ **Day 2:** Memorize Deuteronomy 18:18.

☐ **Day 3:** Read Exodus 2–3. How did Jesus fulfill Moses's purpose?

☐ **Day 4:** What can you determine about Jesus and Moses from John 5:45–47, Acts 13:39, and 1 Corinthians 10:1–4?

☐ **Day 5:** Ask someone at work or school who he or she thinks is the GOAT in sports, movies, music, etc. After that person answers, consider sharing why you believe that Jesus is the greatest leader of all time.

What Is God Looking for in Leaders?

Do not look on his appearance or on the height of his stature, because I have rejected him. For the LORD sees not as man sees: man looks on the outward appearance, but the LORD looks on the heart.

—1 SAMUEL 16:7

I was just a child when President Nixon was impeached. I remember standing in front of a black-and-white TV at our swim club as he announced his resignation. This rocked me even as a kid. I thought, *I can't trust our president, so whom can I trust?* Have you ever been let down by a parent, a pastor, or a politician? Yeah, it's a gut punch for sure. Rather than being critical of others, maybe we should ask ourselves, "If God ever asked me to lead in some capacity, what would he be looking for?" To get to the answer, we need a bit of background.

Rejecting God's Rule

The original plan for the nation of Israel was that God alone would be their king. "The LORD is our judge; the LORD is our lawgiver; the LORD is our king; he will save us" (Isaiah 33:22). So when Israel asked for a king, they were really rejecting God. Samuel was Israel's first major prophet after Moses. When the people asked him to install a king, he was appalled and warned them about the cost of having an earthly monarch. A king would take their sons as soldiers, daughters as servants, and crops as taxes (1 Samuel 8:11–15). Though this was a long time ago, we all know what it's like to trust something other than God—money, power, relationships, or sex.

That God's rule wasn't enough for them should have made them uneasy. Ultimately God permitted a king because the people rejected him. And rejecting God always has serious consequences.

Saul, a Man the People Sought

Israel's first king was a man named Saul. From a human perspective, he had it all. He was tall, strong, and handsome. Plus, his family was rich (1 Samuel 9:1–2). Unfortunately, he tried to rule on his own rather than letting God rule Israel through him. The results were disastrous.

We see these disastrous results when Saul's troops got restless after a battle. He overstepped his authority by personally performing the sacrifice before Samuel arrived (13:8–9). Because of this disobedience, God stripped Saul of his kingdom, even though Saul sat on the throne for nearly forty more years. His dynasty was cut off with these words: "Now your kingdom shall not continue. The LORD has sought out a man after his own heart, and the LORD has commanded him to be prince over his people, because you have not kept what the LORD commanded you" (verse 14). God said to Samuel, "I regret that I have made Saul king, for he has turned back from following me and has not performed my commandments" (15:11).

You see, people's opinions were more important to Saul than God's command. Each time he failed, it was because popular opinion went against God's clear command; Saul promoted himself through manipulation rather than resting on God's approval. Saul forced the results he wanted rather than waiting for God to provide. Then when Saul failed, he blamed someone else. When a leader cannot take responsibility for failure, he's doomed to repeat his mistakes.

Because of Saul's failure, God sent Samuel to anoint a new king. Saul was the right man from a human perspective—tall, strong, capable. Yet none of those qualities qualified him in God's eyes. God looks for a different kind of leader. He instructed Samuel, "Do not look on his appearance or on the height of his stature, because I have rejected him. For the LORD sees not as man sees: man looks on the outward appearance, but the LORD looks on the heart" (16:7; see also 13:14; Acts 13:22).

David, a Man After God's Own Heart

David became the model leader of Israel precisely because he left leadership in God's hands. He was merely God's servant to point God's people to God's laws. His goal was God's fame, not his own. He battled for God's honor, not his own reputation. That's the kind of leader God is looking for. This kind of leadership is, in fact, what he wants from you in your own realm of influence.

David, though imperfect, became the model after which the messianic hopes would be fashioned. His life and legacy point to Jesus. First Samuel 16:7 is a powerful reminder for us to look at the heart of the man, not his appearance.

Jesus, God's True King

Though Jesus claimed a kingdom (Matthew 4:17), he never claimed the title of king. He never gathered a military force or passed laws. He never sat on a throne. Why? Because Jesus thought of himself as king without asserting himself as such during his life on earth. There are two major reasons for this.

First, God is the only true king. Jesus must have been suspicious of any leadership role that resembled the ancient kings of Israel. Since Jesus's primary message was about the kingdom of God, it seems obvious that he was more interested in God's rule than his own.

Second, the monarchy was not God's original political structure for Israel. Although God permitted it, the monarchy appears to have been a necessary evil. Jesus was a descendant of David (2 Samuel 7:12) with a royal role to play. Yet he ruled through submission and sacrifice.

If that's the kind of kingship Jesus envisioned, the Gospels[1] have captured it perfectly. For this reason, we can say that 1 Samuel 16:7 is more a description of Jesus the Messiah than of David the king.

Key Points

- Kingship in Israel was never ideal because it contradicted God's sole rule of Israel.

- Saul's self-promotion forced God to replace him with David, a man who sought God's heart.

- The reason Jesus was the rightful king is that he deflected authority back to God, the only true king of Israel.

This Week

☐ **Day I:** After reading the essay, would you say that you are on track to be the kind of leader God is looking for?

☐ **Day 2:** Memorize 1 Samuel 16:7.

☐ **Day 3:** Read 1 Samuel 15–16. What positive characteristics of David do you have, and which do you need to work on?

☐ **Day 4:** Based on Judges 21:25, 1 Samuel 8:1–18, and 1 Samuel 13:14, what habits should you work on to be God's man or woman?

☐ **Day 5:** Ask a teacher, parent, coach, or other mentor to point out your greatest leadership strength. Ask this person how you could exercise that strength more.

Does God Orchestrate History?

When your days are fulfilled and you lie down with your fathers,
I will raise up your offspring after you, who shall come from your
body, and I will establish his kingdom.

—2 Samuel 7:12

Following a newsfeed may make life seem random. Wars erupt; economies crash; rulers rise and fall. The Bible gives a different impression. God orchestrates events at both the macro and the micro levels. If this statement is true, we can worry less and worship more even during difficult seasons because God's got this! So, let's take a look at one major example of his meticulous direction of world events.

God's Promise of a New David

The greatest king of Israel was a man named David: giant-killer, musician, warrior, lover, friend, and king. The nation loved him, as did God, who promised that David would always have an heir on the throne: "When your days are fulfilled and you lie down with your fathers, I will raise up your offspring after you, who shall come from your body, and I will establish his kingdom. He shall build a house for my name, and I will establish the throne of his kingdom forever" (2 Samuel 7:12–13).

This prediction about David's descendant was recorded elsewhere in the Old Testament (Psalm 89:3–4; Isaiah 11:1) as well as in Jewish writings outside the Bible.

The New Testament writers shared this expectation. The "new David" promise had never been applied to a specific person before, but they claimed that Jesus was its fulfillment.

God's Fulfillment of the Promise in Jesus

Matthew opened the New Testament with a genealogy. Sounds boring, but take a closer look. He did something interesting with it. This former tax collector nerded out a bit with math. He summarized, "All the generations from Abraham to David were *fourteen* generations, and from David to the deportation [exile] to Babylon *fourteen* generations, and from the deportation to Babylon to the Christ *fourteen* generations" (Matthew 1:17). That's 14 + 14 + 14 = Jesus. What does this matter?

In Hebrew, *David* is spelled *DVD*. *D* is the fourth letter of the Hebrew alphabet, and *V* is the sixth. Adding those values, we have 4 + 6 + 4 = 14. This is a very Jewish and very clever way of highlighting Jesus as the fulfillment of God's promise to David.

Even Luke, a Gentile, understood Jesus's connection with King David. The angel Gabriel promised Mary concerning her son, "He will be great and will be called the Son of the Most High. And the Lord God will give to him the throne of his father David" (Luke 1:32). This is why the Messiah had to be born in Bethlehem, the city of David (2:4, 11). It also explains why Jesus entered Jerusalem, the capital city, riding a donkey as other kings did during their coronations (Matthew 21:2–9, 15).

In the first sermon Peter preached after Jesus's resurrection, he reminded his audience that Jesus was David's heir. Peter spoke of David as "knowing that God had sworn with an oath to him that he would set one of his descendants on his throne" (Acts 2:30).

The great apostle Paul, a former rabbi, opened the book of Romans by describing Jesus with these words: "his Son, who was descended from David according to the flesh and was declared to be the Son of God in power according to the Spirit of holiness by his resurrection from the dead, Jesus Christ our Lord" (1:3–4). In his final letter, Paul continued to highlight Jesus's Davidic ancestry: "Remember Jesus Christ, risen from the dead, the offspring of David" (2 Timothy 2:8).

In Revelation John also referred to Jesus's ancestry: "One of the elders said to me, 'Weep no more; behold, the Lion of the tribe of Judah, the Root of David, has conquered'" (5:5). Jesus himself affirmed this aspect of his identity: "I, Jesus, . . . am the root and the descendant of David, the bright morning star" (22:16).

Why Didn't Jesus Claim to Be King?

Since the New Testament makes it clear that Jesus was David's heir, why did Jesus never overtly claim that during his years on earth? The political scene of the triumphal entry and the cleansing of the temple clearly suggests his royal role (Matthew 21:1–16). Likewise, Jesus's calling of twelve apostles looks like the establishment of a political cabinet for Israel's twelve tribes. These actions were clear enough to get him crucified as a would-be king of the Jews. Pilate, the Roman procurator, even inscribed that title on the cross (John 19:19). Yet Jesus never clearly claimed to be king. So, how did he fulfill God's promise of a new King David?

It's in Jesus's humility that he truly modeled David's heart for God. David was anointed king years before sitting on the throne. During those days, he was rejected and maligned, abused and attacked, until Saul's self-destruction inaugurated David's rule over Israel. So, too, for Jesus: suffering and service preceded enthronement because he did *not* assert his rule. God orchestrated history and the crescendo is Jesus:

God has highly exalted him and bestowed on him the name that is above every name, so that at the name of Jesus every knee should bow, in heaven and on earth and under the earth, and every tongue confess that Jesus Christ is Lord, to the glory of God the Father. (Philippians 2:9–11)

Key Points

- God promised David an heir to sit on his throne forever.
- The New Testament claims that Jesus fulfilled that promise.
- Even though Jesus never claimed to be king, God raised him to his rightful throne.

This Week

☐ **Day 1:** Read the essay. In your current season of life, where do you see God directing your life for good?

☐ **Day 2:** Memorize 2 Samuel 7:12.

☐ **Day 3:** In Matthew 21–22, how did Jesus act like a king without making the claim?

☐ **Day 4:** How do Matthew 1:1, Philippians 2:9–11, and Revelation 5:5 show us that Jesus is greater than David?

☐ **Day 5:** Make a list of the ten biggest events of your life. Where do you see God driving, directing, and protecting you?

How Can I Find Happiness?

Blessed is the man
    who walks not in the counsel of the wicked,
nor stands in the way of sinners,
    nor sits in the seat of scoffers;
but his delight is in the law of the LORD,
    and on his law he meditates day and night.

He is like a tree
    planted by streams of water
that yields its fruit in its season,
    and its leaf does not wither.
In all that he does, he prospers.

                —PSALM 1:1–3

We all want to be happy. In fact, we even use happiness as a guide for decisions. You know, "If it feels good, it must be right!" Yet no parent applies this rule to children. Why? Because it can destroy them. To an eight-year-old boy, happiness is skateboarding off the roof into the pool. Not okay. Toddlers are fascinated with electrical outlets and power tools. Not okay. In our teen years, moments of happiness can bring decades of regret. What can we learn from Scripture about God's view of happiness?

God Wants You to Be Happy

God is a good father. And what father doesn't want his kids to be happy? In the Bible, he even tells us how to find happiness.

"Delight yourself in the LORD, and he will give you the desires of your heart" (Psalm 37:4). "Rejoice in the Lord" (Philippians 3:1). "We consider those blessed [happy] who remained steadfast" (James 5:11). The entire book of Ecclesiastes is a discourse on happiness, and you can read Proverbs as a happiness handbook. Here's the takeaway: obedience to God leads to our happiness!

Science of Happiness

When God constructed your brain, he lubricated the synapses with three chemicals of happiness. They're the happy juices of your brain.

Oxytocin is the chemical that creates a sense of safety and trust. It's released through a handshake or a hug.

Dopamine is the chemical of adventure. It's released when your mind is buzzing with activity and creative energy. When you invent a product, write a song, solve a problem, or learn something, you get a dopamine drip.

Serotonin is the chemical of respect. It's released when someone asks your opinion, treats you with respect, or applauds your performance.

Several things are important to understand.

First, these chemicals are highly addictive. That may sound negative, but it's not. God gave you these cravings because he *wants* you to be happy.

Second, these chemicals are short lived. God didn't create you to remain in a long-term state of happiness. Rather, he designed happiness to be dependent on persistent habits that release minibursts of chemicals. God's design leads to long-term habits that build positive communities. It's genius.

Third, happiness is a chemical cocktail that you can control. Here's what I mean . . .

Aside from three chemicals, every human being has three sources of happiness: genetics, circumstances, and choices. Which do you think contributes most to our happiness? According to substantial scientific research, genetics accounts for about half the variation in our happiness.

Circumstances can change our happiness a mere 10 percent. Plus, the highs and lows of circumstances don't last long. On average, any circumstance affects happiness for only ninety days. This leads us to the third source.

Choices like diet, rest, and relationships account for 40 percent of the variance in our happiness.[1] That's statistically huge. You can't control your genetics any more than you can control every circumstance. However, you can control your choices. That means nearly half your overall happiness *is* in your control.

Biblical Happiness

Psalm 1 is the single most important passage in the Bible on happiness. It opens with the keyword *blessed,* the Bible's term for "happy": "Blessed is the man who walks not in the counsel of the wicked, nor stands in the way of sinners, nor sits in the seat of scoffers" (verse 1). If your ambition is true happiness, Psalm 1 is the starting line.

When we build godly relationships, our happiness increases. Friends and family are the best sources of oxytocin. Therefore, above all, choose companions who lead to healthy choices. That's step one.

Step two is to increase dopamine, the discovery chemical. Verse 2 points the way: delight in God's law and meditate on it day and night. The more we meditate on a positive thought, the larger it grows. As we do, we release the addictive dopamine that produces happiness.[2]

Step three is to release serotonin, the chemical of significance. For you and me, being helpful might be the best way to release serotonin. As we serve others, we gain significance. The process is described in verse 3: "He is like a tree planted by streams of water that yields its fruit in its season, and its leaf does not wither. In all that he does, he prospers."

When we're fruitful, we find significance. Simple acts of kindness to people around us will be more effective in giving us the chemical rush of happiness than video games or social media hits.

Psalm 1 reminds us that our choices are more important than our circumstances. Written three thousand years ago, it gives us a clear process for finding happiness: (1) build relationships that honor God, (2) create space in your brain for the truths of God's Word, and (3) serve others in significant ways.

It's that simple and that effective. It doesn't take much. A note of gratitude to a friend, five minutes of meditation on Scripture, or a random act of kindness can release chemicals of happiness in your brain. The small things you do today can build habits that increase happiness for a lifetime.

Key Points

- Your happiness is a chemical cocktail you can control by practicing habits that release oxytocin, dopamine, and serotonin.

- Genetics accounts for 50 percent of the variability in happiness, while circumstances account for another 10 percent. That leaves a whopping 40 percent of our happiness to the choices we make.

- Psalm 1 offers wise counsel about building happiness.

This Week

❑ **Day 1:** Which of the three steps to build happiness do you need to work on first?

❑ **Day 2:** Memorize Psalm 1:1–3.

❑ **Day 3:** Pain is not the opposite of happiness; meaninglessness is. Read Job 1–2 with this truth in mind. How is pain often a prerequisite for meaning?

❑ **Day 4:** How would you use Psalm 37:4, Philippians 3:1, and 1 Thessalonians 5:16 to answer the question "Does God want me to be happy?"

❑ **Day 5:** On your phone or on paper, list the alphabet. Now write one quality or gift God has given you to match each letter.

10

Is There Proof That Jesus Is God's Son?

> You are my Son;
> today I have begotten you.
>
> —PSALM 2:7

Have you ever had friends who got so lovestruck over a new crush that they couldn't stop gushing? To hear them talk, absolutely *everything* about this new love interest is *the* best and *the* most attractive. Their crush is *the* most amazing person *ever*!

Sweet at first, right? But if your friend doesn't calm down and get some perspective, eventually you're likely to bust out with "Come on! No one is *that* perfect!"

Crushing hard, then crashing hard often happens to lovers. Likewise, mentors and leaders can let you down. The more important the person in our lives, the clearer we'd better be on who that person really is. That's why if we are going to devote our lives to Jesus, we need to ask, Who is he *really*? *Is* there reliable evidence that Jesus is God's son?

Evidence from Psalm 2 That Jesus Is God's Son

God himself paraphrased this chapter's core verse twice during Jesus's ministry. At Jesus's baptism, God spoke in a voice audible to the crowd. The Holy Spirit then affirmed God's declaration by descending in the form of a dove (Matthew 3:16–17). It was a *big* deal. The second time was in the middle of Jesus's three-year ministry, when he was transfigured on a high mountain in the presence of Moses and Elijah (17:1–8). In one sense, this event marked the peak of Jesus's earthly existence. It was the closest he ever got to sharing God's glory while on this globe.

With these statements, God didn't just show his approval. He affirmed Jesus as the rightful heir to the throne of Israel. A thousand years before Jesus was born, the Bible predicted a coming Messiah. *Messiah* means "anointed one," in reference to a king's coronation. Israel's Messiah was to sit on David's throne, rescue Israel as Moses did, and bless all nations as Abraham's offspring. As God's ruler, he would bring God's rescue and God's blessing to God's people.

Psalm 2:7 is just one of dozens of major messianic prophecies that identified who this Savior-King would be. They told where he would be born (Micah 5:2), how he would die (Isaiah 53:3–5), the price of his betrayal (Zechariah 11:12), and the nature of his ministry (Isaiah 61:1). Christians have always seen Jesus as the figure to fulfill this broad array of prophecies. No one else fulfilled these predictions. And there's not even a close second.

In fact, Jesus is the only individual in the past two thousand years to successfully claim the title of Messiah. With that fact in mind, let's return to Psalm 2. This psalm contains not one messianic prophecy but three. First, verses 1–2 identify four groups—nations, peoples, kings, and rulers—that were the very players in the drama of Jesus's final week on earth: Gentiles, Jewish people, Herod, and Pilate (Acts 4:25–27). While many rabbis would deny that this was the correct interpretation, they could hardly deny that the descriptions fit like a glove.

Second, verse 7 of Psalm 2 is paraphrased in the first three gospels at both Jesus's baptism (Matthew 3:17; Mark 1:11; Luke 3:22) and his transfiguration (Matthew 17:5; Mark 9:7; Luke 9:35). What makes this fact an even bigger deal is that God spoke audibly only three times during Jesus's ministry, and twice he paraphrased this verse.

Third, Psalm 2:9—"You shall break them with a rod of iron and dash them in pieces like a potter's vessel"—is referred to three times in Revelation (2:27; 12:5; 19:15) to describe Jesus's royal rule.

Per square inch, there's hardly a passage with more messianic meaning than Psalm 2. But Psalm 2 is only the beginning! Many passages are loaded with messianic promises (see Psalm 110; 118; Isaiah 53; Daniel 7; Zechariah 11–12).

Prophetic Evidence That Jesus Is God's Son

Throughout the Old Testament, there are more than sixty major prophecies concerning the coming Messiah. Here are some examples:

1. He would be born in Bethlehem (Micah 5:2).
2. He would be preceded by a messenger (Malachi 3:1).
3. He would enter Jerusalem while riding a donkey (Zechariah 9:9).
4. He would be betrayed by a friend, which would result in his back being wounded (Zechariah 13:6).
5. He would be sold for thirty pieces of silver, which would be given to a potter (Zechariah 11:12–13).
6. He would stand silent before his oppressors (Isaiah 53:7).
7. He would die by crucifixion (Psalm 22:16).

Some of these predictions are very specific and unexpected. Most would be impossible to manipulate or prearrange (such as where someone is born). Together, these prophecies are almost impossible to ignore.

Peter Stoner, in *Science Speaks,* calculated the probability of these passages being fulfilled by one man to be only 1 in 100,000,000,000,000,000— that's one in *one hundred quadrillion!*[1]

One hundred quadrillion is an incomprehensibly large number. To put the odds in perspective, Stoner gave an illustration. He said it would be like covering the state of Texas two feet deep in silver dollars, with one of those silver dollars painted red, then asking a blindfolded volunteer to wander across the state and randomly select one of the coins. His odds of picking the red one are the same as the odds of Jesus randomly fulfilling just these seven predictions.[2]

If we're going to deny that Jesus is the Messiah, we owe ourselves an explanation as to how one man could have randomly fulfilled so many detailed prophecies.

Perhaps you're a skeptic. Fair enough. Any single prophecy could be explained away, I suppose. But the cumulative effect, the weight of the whole, is a firm foundation on which to stand.

Key Points

- Only Jesus has successfully claimed to be the Messiah.

- Psalm 2 is a particularly influential messianic prophecy because of its three separate predictions cited in the New Testament.

- Messianic prophecies are compelling evidence for Jesus because they're so specific and because so many are impossible to fulfill on purpose.

This Week

☐ **Day 1:** What evidence from this essay gives you the most compelling reason to believe that Jesus is God's son?

☐ **Day 2:** Memorize Psalm 2:7.

☐ **Day 3:** Since we're talking about prophecy, let's read part of the biography of the most famous prophet, Elijah (1 Kings 18–19). Was he the kind of person you could count on to tell the truth?

☐ **Day 4:** What evidence do we find in Psalm 22:1, Psalm 118:22–29, and Revelation 19:15 that Jesus is God's son?

☐ **Day 5:** Have a conversation with your parents or guardians. Ask, "What gives *you* confidence that Jesus is really who he says he is?" If they aren't believers, consider asking why. Listen respectfully, and be ready to tell them why you have confidence in Jesus.

11

Is God Really Watching Out for Me?

The LORD is my shepherd; I shall not want.

He makes me lie down in green pastures.

He leads me beside still waters.

He restores my soul.

—PSALM 23:1–3

After my parents' divorce, I experienced an unsettling feeling of insecurity. They did the best they could, but for me as a twelve-year-old, it was traumatic. After that, I just didn't know whom to trust or where to turn. Most people, at various points in life, experience the same feeling. Perhaps that's why "The LORD is my shepherd" (Psalm 23:1) strikes a chord with so many.

Maybe you are going through a difficult time right now. If so, it is strong comfort to know that even when you're in the valley of the shadow of death, under discipline, or in the presence of your enemies (verses 4–5), God is working for your good. No passage in the Bible conveys that truth as powerfully and beautifully as Psalm 23.

Leaders as Shepherds

God expects his leaders to act as shepherds. Like a shepherd's, their power is for protection. Their rods and staffs are for guidance. The shepherd sacrifices for the sheep, not the sheep for the shepherd. The qualities of a shepherd are obvious in the life of David, the great shepherd-king who penned this psalm and who came to prominence by slaying a giant with a shepherd's sling (1 Samuel 17:40–50).

In fact, David's time in the field was his best preparation for the throne. We read,

> [God] chose David his servant
>   and took him from the sheepfolds;
> from following the nursing ewes he brought him
>   to shepherd Jacob his people,
>   Israel his inheritance.
> With upright heart he shepherded them
>   and guided them with his skillful hand. (Psalm 78:70–72)

The same could be said of Moses (Exodus 3:1; Psalm 77:20; Isaiah 63:11). Forty years in the wilderness tending sheep prepared him for forty years of leading Israel through the desert. And before Moses, there was Abraham (Genesis 13:2–6), who was famed for the size of his flocks.

Because the heroes of Israel's past were literal shepherds, leaders throughout her history were compared to shepherds. This was true for kings, governors, prophets, and priests (1 Kings 22:17; Jeremiah 10:21; 17:16).

The Lord as Shepherd

Notice how the prophets predicted that a new king like David would come to lead Israel: "I will set up over them one shepherd, my servant David, and he shall feed them: he shall feed them and be their shepherd" (Ezekiel 34:23).

Jesus's status as the promised shepherd-king is clear from his birth in Bethlehem (Micah 5:2–4, cited in Matthew 2:6) to his death in Jerusalem (Zechariah 13:7, cited in Matthew 26:31; Mark 14:27; John 16:32).

Jesus said he would judge people, separating them like sheep and goats (Matthew 25:32). In John 10:1–18, he critiqued the false shepherds as the prophets of old had done. When Mark wrote that the crowds waiting for Jesus were like "sheep without a shepherd" (Mark 6:34), he was alluding to Moses's description of Joshua as a leader who would keep Israel from being like "sheep that have no shepherd" (Numbers 27:17). Joshua led Israel into the Promised Land; Jesus would lead God's people into a new kind of promised land. What's more? Jesus's name, in Hebrew, is "Joshua."

Three New Testament authors referred to Jesus's role as shepherd: "May the God of peace who brought again from the dead our Lord Jesus, the great shepherd of the sheep, by the blood of the eternal covenant, equip you with everything good that you may do his will" (Hebrews 13:20–21). "You were straying like sheep, but have now returned to the Shepherd and Overseer of your souls" (1 Peter 2:25). "The Lamb in the midst of the throne will be their shepherd, and he will guide them to springs of living water, and God will wipe away every tear from their eyes" (Revelation 7:17).

By the end of the Bible, the shepherd of Psalm 23 has a new name, a new face, and a new mailing address. Jesus is God in a human body. He lived among us to lay down his life for his sheep. That's just what the Good Shepherd does.

In fact, in an unexpected twist, the Good Shepherd is also the Lamb of God. His sacrifice at Passover permanently replaced the Jewish sacrificial system. During the first Passover, a lamb belonged to the Lord as a replacement for the firstborn son. Jesus is our substitute to cover all our sins. He is the once-and-for-all perfect Passover sacrifice.

This had, in fact, been God's plan all along. Psalm 23, the song of the Shepherd, is preceded by Psalm 22, the song of the Lamb—the clearest description of Calvary outside the Gospels.

Leadership is no longer what you get *from* the sheep but what you sacrifice *for* the sheep. Consequently, any Christian who picks up the staff of leadership also accepts the rod of suffering. Apostles, evangelists, and pastors (Ephesians 4:11), along with elders (Acts 20:28–29; 1 Peter 5:2–3), have the privilege of leading and feeding the sheep if they're willing to lay down their lives for the sheep.

Jesus set the example for us. Those who don't know the Good Shepherd often find this profound truth unbelievable: our God suffered on our behalf.

Key Points

- Any who rule on God's behalf must act as shepherds.

- Jesus is not only the promised shepherd-king but also the perfect Passover lamb.

- Church leaders—apostles, evangelists, pastors, elders—take up the mantle of shepherds.

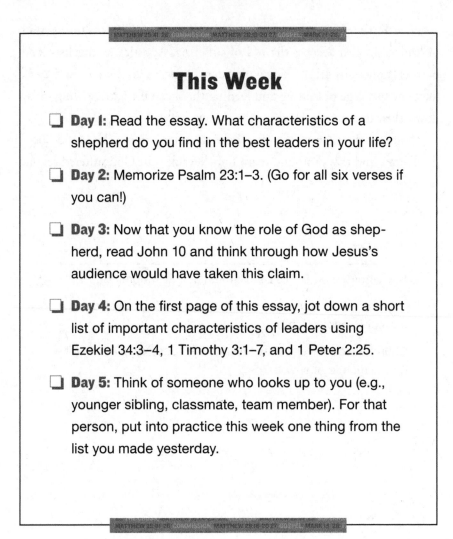

This Week

☐ **Day 1:** Read the essay. What characteristics of a shepherd do you find in the best leaders in your life?

☐ **Day 2:** Memorize Psalm 23:1–3. (Go for all six verses if you can!)

☐ **Day 3:** Now that you know the role of God as shepherd, read John 10 and think through how Jesus's audience would have taken this claim.

☐ **Day 4:** On the first page of this essay, jot down a short list of important characteristics of leaders using Ezekiel 34:3–4, 1 Timothy 3:1–7, and 1 Peter 2:25.

☐ **Day 5:** Think of someone who looks up to you (e.g., younger sibling, classmate, team member). For that person, put into practice this week one thing from the list you made yesterday.

12

Is Jesus a Real Savior?

The LORD says to my Lord:
"Sit at my right hand,
until I make your enemies your footstool."

—PSALM 110:1

My two brothers are pretty goofy. I love them, but if one of them claimed to be my savior? Yeah, right! That's why it's so impressive that two of Jesus's brothers eventually proclaimed him as Lord. And it wasn't just his brothers; many of the Jewish leaders became convinced. Let's eavesdrop on one of the earliest debates about Jesus's identity.

Jesus was in the temple in Jerusalem on the Tuesday before he died. It had been a full day of debates, with his opponents sending experts to trap him with questions. For hours, they grilled him with tough theological questions, and his answers totally blew them away (Matthew 21:23–22:40)!

Jesus's Use of Psalm 110

Then Jesus asked a question of his own based on Psalm 110:1: "What do you think about the Christ? Whose son is he?" (Matthew 22:42). It should have been easy enough to answer: Who is the Christ in Psalm 110? Surely the national religious leaders could explain their position. After all, this was a famous passage.

What happened next often gets lost on those of us outside Jewish culture. Here are two clarifications that will help.

First, when reading, "The LORD says to my Lord" (verse 1), you might notice in the English translation that the first "LORD" is in small caps. Why? Because it's a different Hebrew word. The Hebrew literally says, "Yahweh (LORD) said to my Adonai (Lord)." Clearly *Yahweh* is a reference to God. *Adonai,* however, could refer to either God or a human dignitary. So, which is it? Was Jesus claiming to be divine or just the human descendant of David?

Second, in Jewish culture, the father was always greater than the son. So, if the Messiah (or Christ) was a descendant of David, who is greater? Even though the forefather was always greater, that's not what David wrote. He said the Messiah was *his* Lord. How is that possible?

That was Jesus's question: "If then David calls him Lord, how is he his son?" (Matthew 22:45). His hearers had no answer: "No one was able to answer him a word," the Bible says, "nor from that day did anyone dare to ask him any more questions" (verse 46). Boom! Sort of a mic-drop moment for Jesus!

The leaders were stunned because they couldn't imagine incarnation (God becoming flesh in Jesus). If God couldn't become flesh, David's statement would be nonsense. However, if God did become flesh, the entire poem comes into focus. Two statements make sense only in the context of incarnation.

The first is "Sit at my right hand" (Psalm 110:1). God's right hand is a position of divine power (Daniel 7:13–14; Matthew 26:64). If Jesus is not divine, he could not be placed at God's right hand. But this is where he *always* is after the Ascension: "The Lord Jesus, after he had spoken to them, was taken up into heaven and sat down at the right hand of God" (Mark 16:19; see also Luke 22:69; Acts 5:31; 7:55; Romans 8:34; Hebrews 1:3).

The second, which also suggests deity (that Jesus is God in the flesh), is "You are a priest forever after the order of Melchizedek" (Psalm 110:4).

But wait. Melchize-*who*?

This mysterious figure appears in the story of Abraham. He honored Melchizedek, the king of Salem, with a tenth of the spoils of war (Genesis 14:17–20). Melchizedek in Judaism is like Santa Claus in the West. He had a real history, but his legend is greater by far. This king of a Canaanite city was somehow also a priest of the Most High God. However, king and priest were *separate* vocations in Judaism. The Davidic kings and the Aaronic priests ran on two different tracks. Which meant if a Jewish king were to also be a priest, his qualifications for priesthood would have to come from a completely separate lineage. Enter Melchizedek. As both king and priest, he foreshadowed Jesus, our Messiah.

Only Jesus has ever fulfilled Psalm 110. He's a human descendant of David—a king in a royal lineage. But he's also a high priest in the lineage of Melchizedek. Jesus made this claim himself, and Peter repeated it on the Day of Pentecost near the very spot where Jesus had earlier recited the verse: "David did not ascend into the heavens, but he himself says, 'The Lord said to my Lord, "Sit at my right hand, until I make your enemies your footstool"'" (Acts 2:34–35).

Paul followed suit. Three times he alluded to Psalm 110, declaring that Jesus is at the right hand of God (Romans 8:34; Ephesians 1:20; Colossians 3:1). The author of Hebrews agreed, placing Jesus at God's right hand as co-ruler (Hebrews 1:3; 8:1; 10:12; 12:2). The unanimous voice in the New Testament is that Jesus fulfilled the prophecy of Psalm 110. No other individual fits the description. Jesus alone can claim to be God's son and David's Adonai.

Here's our takeaway: *Jesus is God's king, ruling with authority. Jesus is also our high priest, enabling us to connect with almighty God.*

Once, Jesus asked his friends, "Who do you say that I am?" Peter replied, "You are the Christ, the Son of the living God" (Matthew 16:15–16). Peter got it! Ecstatic, Jesus answered, "Blessed are you, Simon Bar-Jonah! For flesh and blood has not revealed this to you, but my Father who is in heaven" (verse 17).

The same question is posed to us: "Who do *you* say Jesus is?" It's the single most important question you will ever answer.

Key Points

- The Messiah (or Christ) was an earthly king predicted by the Jews.

- Only the incarnation of Jesus fulfills Psalm 110.

- After the Resurrection, Jesus ascended to the right hand of God, as predicted by Psalm 110.

This Week

☐ **Day 1:** On the first page of the essay, make a brief list of the evidence that convinces you that Jesus really is our Savior.

☐ **Day 2:** Memorize Psalm 110:1.

☐ **Day 3:** As you talk to people about Jesus, not every-one will be convinced. Read John 5–6, looking for similarities between the objections Jesus encountered here and the ones he faced in Matthew 21–22.

☐ **Day 4:** Look for the ways people reacted to Jesus's claims in Matthew 16:16–18, Matthew 22:41–46, and Acts 2:34-37.

☐ **Day 5:** Write out a prayer. Praise Jesus for his power, or call out to him for help. As Messiah, he is both your powerful king and your compassionate priest.

13

If Jesus Was Rejected Back Then, Why Should I Accept Him Now?

> The stone that the builders rejected
> has become the cornerstone.
>
> —PSALM 118:22

In our culture, it's getting less and less popular to be a Christian. We are called hypocrites and bigots, and who wants to be called that? But just because something is unpopular doesn't make it wrong. In fact, if a broken world is upside down, then being countercultural may just be right side up. That's actually an old argument that Jesus himself used when he quoted Psalm 118:22. He quoted it during his final debate in the temple (Mark 12:10), and his example was followed by Peter (Acts 4:11; 1 Peter 2:7) and Paul (Ephesians 2:20). Let's take a closer look.

The Psalm

Psalm 118 was not foreign soil for the scribes. They wrote about it in what they called the Targum, an ancient paraphrase of the Bible. It includes a curious variation that apparently predates Jesus: "The *boy* the builders rejected; he was among the *sons of Jesse* and he was privileged to be appointed as king and ruler."[1] Why on earth would they change "stone" to "son"? Well, these two words in Hebrew are almost identical. "Son" is *ben;* "stone" is *eben.* A simple sound at the beginning of the word turns the boy into a stone. In other words, the Targum makes a play on words that helps interpret the verse. God's foundation stone turned out to be a person, not a rock.

Well, that makes sense. God's kingdom is built on people, not property. Furthermore, the person on whom the nation would stand was to be King David's descendant, or as the Targum phrases it, "among the sons of Jesse."

Therefore, long before Jesus, the rabbis understood that the prophesied Messiah would be rejected in his day. God would, however, reverse the rejection by using it to establish his son in the most important role in the nation.

The Parable

Jesus cited Psalm 118:22 in his parable about a vineyard (Matthew 21:33–44). It's a classic story of bad guys whom every listener would want to see taken out. And then Jesus concluded it with a quote that converts the story from fiction to biography: "The stone that the builders rejected has become the cornerstone" (verse 42). This single sentence, plucked from the prophetic psalm, describes the plan of God. Jesus's execution by the leaders of Israel would result in the nation's salvation. The divine irony is thick.

For the religious leaders in Jesus's audience, this parable must have felt like a gut punch. They had planned his death to prove he was *not* the Messiah. Jesus used Scripture to show how his death would prove he *was* the Messiah.

Jesus said, "I tell you, the kingdom of God will be taken away from you and given to a people producing its fruits. And the one who falls on this stone will be broken to pieces; and when it falls on anyone, it will crush him" (verses 43–44). Jesus is brilliant! He took their attempt to discredit him and turned it into evidence in his favor.

Talk about flipping the script! This must have been maddening to the Jewish leaders. Their response is predictable: "When the chief priests and the Pharisees heard his parables, they perceived that he was speaking about them. And although they were seeking to arrest him, they feared the crowds, because they held him to be a prophet" (verses 45–46).

The Apostles and the Psalm

A month and a half later, we land in Acts 4. It was after Jesus's resurrection. Peter and John had been arrested for healing a man who couldn't walk (3:1–8). Peter defended their action by referring to—you guessed it— Psalm 118:22: "This Jesus is the stone that was rejected by you, the builders, which has become the cornerstone" (Acts 4:11). If you were Peter—outgunned and outnumbered—wouldn't *you* mimic Jesus by referencing the very passage he'd used to silence his opponents? It worked! Game, set, match. Of course, insulting the judge when you're on trial may not be your best play. Even so, Peter wasn't trying to convince the judge; he was winning over the crowd.

Jesus's rejection back then is not a reason for anyone to reject him now, because the rejection back then was not the end of the story. Jesus is the cornerstone, and the next verses of Psalm 118 celebrate the Messiah's victory over sin and death. The prophetic psalm points out that God saw this victory coming.

Paul also used this psalm. In his letter to the Ephesians, he argued for the unity of all ethnic groups based on the power of Jesus's death and resurrection:

Through him we both have access in one Spirit to the Father. So then you are no longer strangers and aliens, but you are fellow citizens with the saints and members of the household of God, built on the foundation of the apostles and prophets, *Christ Jesus himself being the cornerstone.* (2:18–20)

This is huge! We have access to God because Jesus died in our place. After his humiliation (crucifixion), God exalted him (resurrection) as Savior and Lord. The same pattern is true for us. When we humble ourselves, God lifts us up (James 4:10). What does that mean? Through Jesus we're accepted. Through Jesus we're forgiven. We now have a place in God's kingdom—his church. Like Jesus's, our road might be paved with trials and tears, but because we're in him, God will lift us up in the end.

Key Points

- Some rabbis around the time of Jesus interpreted this stone as the offspring of King David.

- Jesus's parable of the vineyard is actually Israel's history and a picture of his establishment as king.

- The biblical principle of humiliation coming before exaltation played out in Jesus's death and resurrection.

This Week

☐ **Day 1:** As you read the essay, can you think of anything else that was unpopular but turned out to be right?

☐ **Day 2:** Memorize Psalm 118:22.

☐ **Day 3:** Read the entire story of Peter quoting Psalm 118:22 in front of the Sanhedrin (Acts 3–4).

☐ **Day 4:** Think about these countercultural passages that turned out to be true: Isaiah 7:14, Matthew 21:33–46, and Acts 4:11.

☐ **Day 5:** Identify one popular thing you need to stop doing because it isn't right.

How Do I Become Wise?

The fear of the LORD is the beginning of knowledge;
fools despise wisdom and instruction.

—PROVERBS 1:7

When I was a teenager, I wanted to be popular. When I was a young man, I wanted to be respected. Now I'm in a season of life when those things matter much less. I just want to be wise. What do *you* want?

Just for a moment, use your imagination to race ahead on the road of life. Ask yourself, "What would it take to be known then as a person of wisdom?"

Wisdom in the Bible

Wisdom for many today evokes an image of Yoda or a guru sitting cross-legged and pondering the mysteries of the universe. For the Jews of the Bible, wisdom was more bolted to everyday experience. Wisdom in the Bible is the ability to practically live out God's truths in ways that bring health to us, our families, and our communities. It's the skills a builder needs to construct a house, a general needs to win a war, and a father needs to raise his children.

Jesus stood squarely in that tradition of wisdom in action. Responding to his critics, he said, "The Son of Man came eating and drinking, and they say, 'Look at him! A glutton and a drunkard, a friend of tax collectors and sinners!' *Yet wisdom is justified by her deeds*" (Matthew 11:19).

The most famous Jewish sage was Solomon. When he became king, God invited him to ask for anything (2 Chronicles 1:7). Here's how Solomon responded: "Give me now wisdom and knowledge to go out and come in before this people, for who can govern this people of yours, which is so great?" (verse 10). God's answer was a resounding yes: "God gave Solomon wisdom and understanding beyond measure, and breadth of mind like the sand on the seashore" (1 Kings 4:29).

Wisdom is a gift of the Spirit. It's not lifeless knowledge but the living, breathing Spirit within us. Wisdom is when the Spirit of God guides a person for God's good (Deuteronomy 34:9; Isaiah 11:2; Acts 6:3, 10; 1 Corinthians 2:13; Ephesians 1:17; Colossians 1:9).

Take Solomon as an example. When he asked for wisdom, God gave himself—the abiding presence of the Spirit to help Solomon lead God's nation.

Was Solomon the wisest man who ever lived? Or would that be Jesus?

The title fits both of them in one sense. However, if we get technical, Solomon was the wisest man, while Jesus is wisdom itself. While Solomon had wisdom because the Spirit was with him, Jesus *is* wisdom because he shares the same essence as the Spirit. This is why Paul could say that "Christ [is] the power of God and the wisdom of God" (1 Corinthians 1:24) and that in Jesus "are hidden all the treasures of wisdom and knowledge" (Colossians 2:3).

Let's press Pause here and turn to *fear*, the other keyword of Proverbs 1:7.

Fear of the Lord

If God is love, why in the world would we fear him? Doesn't the Bible say that "perfect love casts out fear" (1 John 4:18)?

No Christian should fear punishment, since Christ paid our debt. Nor should we fear failure, since God is with us no matter what happens. However, fear and love are not opposites. You might remember when you were a kid and your father "threw you to the moon." The very strength that launched you into the air also comforted you in the dark. So it is with our Father in heaven: "As a father shows compassion to his children, so the LORD shows compassion to those who fear him" (Psalm 103:13).

What do I do when I fear someone? The answer is easy: I obey that person. "Now, Israel, what does the LORD your God require of you, but to *fear* the LORD your God, to *walk* in all his ways, to *love* him, to *serve* the LORD your God with all your heart and with all your soul?" (Deuteronomy 10:12). If you both fear and love someone, then honoring that person with obedience is your natural response (Job 28:28; Psalm 111:10).

The Advantage of Fearing God

"Fear God" isn't the most popular command of the Bible. Yet fearing God offers a number of advantages. Fearing God makes you *fearless.* The Bible includes hundreds of verses about fear. But God's people are told to fear only two things: God and nothing. "You shall not fear them, for it is the LORD your God who fights for you" (Deuteronomy 3:22). Again and again we're encouraged to be fearless. Why? Because once we fear God, there's nothing left to fear.

Along with the fear of the Father comes the *comfort* of the Spirit: "The church throughout all Judea and Galilee and Samaria had peace and was being built up. And walking in the *fear* of the Lord and in the *comfort* of the Holy Spirit, it multiplied" (Acts 9:31).

Fear also produces *holiness:* "Since we have these promises, beloved, let us cleanse ourselves from every defilement of body and spirit, bringing holiness to completion in the fear of God" (2 Corinthians 7:1). And fear fosters *health:* "The fear of the LORD prolongs life, but the years of the wicked will be short" (Proverbs 10:27). And again, "The fear of the LORD is a fountain of life, that one may turn away from the snares of death" (14:27).

Finally, *fearing God* and *praise for God* go hand in hand (Psalm 22:23, 25; 40:3; Revelation 19:5). Fear turns to reverence; reverence, to awe; and awe, to adoration. Our praise rises not merely by feelings of love but by honor rooted in fear of God's power, majesty, and holiness.

Key Points

- Wisdom is the practical ability to succeed at life.

- Fear of the Lord is like respect for fathers—it is not the opposite of love.

- Fear of the Lord is demonstrated by obedience to his commands.

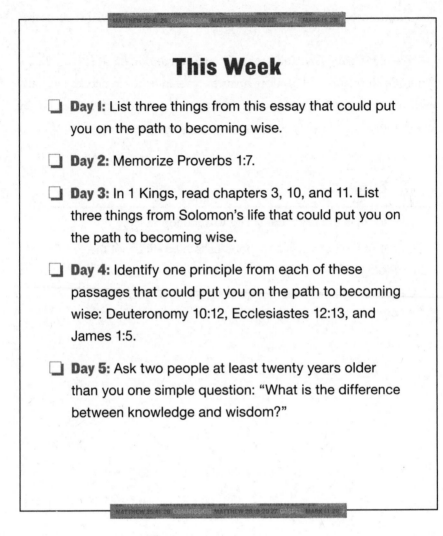

This Week

☐ **Day 1:** List three things from this essay that could put you on the path to becoming wise.

☐ **Day 2:** Memorize Proverbs 1:7.

☐ **Day 3:** In 1 Kings, read chapters 3, 10, and 11. List three things from Solomon's life that could put you on the path to becoming wise.

☐ **Day 4:** Identify one principle from each of these passages that could put you on the path to becoming wise: Deuteronomy 10:12, Ecclesiastes 12:13, and James 1:5.

☐ **Day 5:** Ask two people at least twenty years older than you one simple question: "What is the difference between knowledge and wisdom?"

How Can Jesus's Death Take Care of My Problems?

> He was pierced for our transgressions;
> he was crushed for our iniquities;
> upon him was the chastisement that brought us peace,
> and with his wounds we are healed.
>
> —ISAIAH 53:5

If you were to get to know me, you would see I'm a pretty independent person. I want to make my own way. In the words of a two-year-old, "I do it myself!" Maybe you're like that too. I'll admit, this attitude has made it difficult for me to accept that Jesus died for me. As much as I've tried, however, I just can't fix myself. I need his help.

The fancy church word for what Jesus did for us is *atonement*.[1] You'll run across that now and again in Scripture and sermons. Over half of its uses in the Bible are in a single book—Leviticus—where it describes the role of a sacrifice to cover the sins of the people. Atonement basically means that you owed a debt and somebody else paid it for you.

According to Scripture, sin carries a penalty of death: "The life of the flesh is in the blood, and I have given it for you on the altar to make atonement for your souls, for it is the blood that makes atonement by the life" (Leviticus 17:11). To recover our relationship with God, a blood sacrifice has to be made. These days, that idea can seem barbaric. Think about it, though: Why would our human evaluation of sin's cost hold much weight, particularly when we've been poisoned by our own pride and Satan's seductions?

Perhaps our response to this biblical truth should be submission more than critique. Let me show you three ideas embedded in Isaiah 53 that help us better understand this grand theme of atonement in the Bible.

Great Surprise of Isaiah 53 for Modern America

Atonement is collective, not just individual. Whether we realize it or not, our own nation is experiencing unprecedented levels of moral bankruptcy. It's not just me who's in need of a Savior; it's "we the people." Our communities, our churches, and our nation could use a good bit of saving.

This chapter describes how the servant suffers on behalf of the nation and brings healing to God's people. It was clear in the Old Testament and should be today: we need a Savior. What wasn't clear until Isaiah prophesied was that such a Savior would suffer on behalf of his people rather than causing suffering for his enemies.

Enter Jesus. He was a very different kind of Savior. His salvation wasn't merely personal; it was national. He was rescuing not an individual but an entire nation.

Great Surprise of Isaiah 53 for Ancient Israel

This idea that the Savior would suffer turned the normal Jewish perspective on its head. In Judaism, the wicked were supposed to be sacrificed—"a ransom for the righteous" (Proverbs 21:18). The Jews believed that the

Messiah was to save Israel with power, not suffering. He was to dish out the pain, not absorb it himself.

What Israel had to learn was that their Messiah was a suffering servant. What we must remember is that our Savior is our king.

Great Fulfillment of Isaiah 53 in Jesus

Isaiah 52:13–53:12 is a song about God's suffering servant. It is full of predictions about Jesus's life, death, and resurrection:

- "His appearance was so marred, beyond human semblance" (52:14)—this fits the description of his brutal beatings.
- "He had no form or majesty that we should look at him" (53:2)—this was true of a peasant carpenter.
- "He was despised and rejected by men" (verse 3)—this was true during his execution.
- "He has borne our griefs and carried our sorrows. . . . He was pierced for our transgressions; . . . with his wounds we are healed. . . . The LORD has laid on him the iniquity of us all. . . . [He was] like a lamb that is led to the slaughter, . . . stricken for the transgression of my people" (verses 4–8)—these are descriptions of the Cross.
- "They made his grave with the wicked and with a rich man in his death" (verse 9)—this is a poetic juxtaposition of the criminals crucified beside Jesus and of the tomb of Joseph of Arimathea in which Jesus was buried.
- "When his soul makes an offering for guilt, he shall see his offspring; he shall prolong his days; the will of the LORD shall prosper in his hand" (verse 10)—these statements predict the resurrection of Jesus.
- "By his knowledge shall the righteous one, my servant, make many to be accounted righteous, and he shall bear their iniqui-

ties" (verse 11)—this describes Jesus's substitutionary atonement.

Jesus saw himself as the suffering servant of Isaiah 53. In fact, he spoke of that role as his life mission: "Even the Son of Man came not to be served but to serve, and to give his life as a ransom for many" (Mark 10:45). This verse echoes Isaiah 53:11: "Out of the anguish of his soul he shall see and be satisfied; by his knowledge shall the righteous one, my servant, make many to be accounted righteous, and he shall bear their iniquities."

Mark 10:45 is not alone. Not counting James and Jude, every New Testament author describes the substitutionary effect of Jesus's death (Matthew 20:28; John 11:49–52; Acts 20:28; Romans 3:23–25; 2 Corinthians 5:14–15; Galatians 3:13–14; 1 Timothy 2:5–6; Titus 2:14; Hebrews 9:22, 28; 1 Peter 1:18–19; 1 John 2:2; Revelation 5:9). Paul famously wrote, "The wages of sin is death, but the free gift of God is eternal life in Christ Jesus our Lord" (Romans 6:23).

There's a clear and unified voice in the New Testament: *through Jesus's suffering and death, the penalty of our sin was paid.* That is atonement in action, and that's why we can live in freedom from sin.

Key Points

- Atonement is a necessary sacrifice of blood for our sins.
- Jesus sacrificed his life to save a nation, not merely individuals.
- Jesus's suffering bought our freedom.

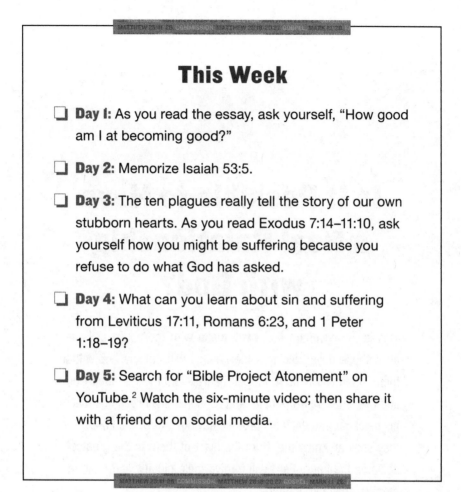

This Week

☐ **Day 1:** As you read the essay, ask yourself, "How good am I at becoming good?"

☐ **Day 2:** Memorize Isaiah 53:5.

☐ **Day 3:** The ten plagues really tell the story of our own stubborn hearts. As you read Exodus 7:14–11:10, ask yourself how you might be suffering because you refuse to do what God has asked.

☐ **Day 4:** What can you learn about sin and suffering from Leviticus 17:11, Romans 6:23, and 1 Peter 1:18–19?

☐ **Day 5:** Search for "Bible Project Atonement" on YouTube.[2] Watch the six-minute video; then share it with a friend or on social media.

Is It Possible to Have a Real Relationship with God?

This is the covenant that I will make with the house of Israel after those days, declares the LORD: I will put my law within them, and I will write it on their hearts. And I will be their God, and they shall be my people. And no longer shall each one teach his neighbor and each his brother, saying, "Know the LORD," for they shall all know me, from the least of them to the greatest, declares the LORD. For I will forgive their iniquity, and I will remember their sin no more.

—JEREMIAH 31:33–34

I was baptized on my ninth birthday. I remember vividly the feeling of warmth that came over me and the heightened awareness that God was with me. I called out to him and he came to me. What I've come to learn since—and it was in the Bible all along—is that long before we call out to God, he seeks us out for relationship. That is the promise he made thousands of years ago through Jeremiah.

The Need for a New Covenant

Jeremiah was known as the weeping prophet—and for good reason. He constantly suffered for saying what God told him to say. And so much of what God told him about Jerusalem's future was absolutely heartbreaking.

Through all Jeremiah's tears and above all his dark prophecies shone a single ray of light. We see it in Jeremiah 31:31–34, which predicts a new and better covenant for God's people.

With these words, Jeremiah expressed one of the deepest longings of Israel. God's people loved God's law, but they just couldn't keep it. They kept sinning, kept sacrificing, and kept suffering for their rebellion. They needed to replace rule keeping with a relationship with God.

Two other prophets said essentially the same thing.

Ezekiel 36:26–27: "I will give you a new heart, and a new spirit I will put within you. And I will remove the heart of stone from your flesh and give you a heart of flesh. And I will put my Spirit within you, and cause you to walk in my statutes and be careful to obey my rules."

Joel 2:28, 32:

> It shall come to pass afterward,
>> that I will pour out my Spirit on all flesh;
> your sons and your daughters shall prophesy,
>> your old men shall dream dreams,
>> and your young men shall see visions. . . .

> And it shall come to pass that everyone who calls on the name of the LORD shall be saved.

Bottom line: the Jews were experiencing the failure of the old covenant of Moses.

Advantages of the New Covenant

Jeremiah promised a better covenant. Everyone would know God personally. All people would have equal access to God—men and women, old and young, rich and poor, of all nations, ethnicities, and political affiliations. We can now approach God confidently *and directly* without a go-between. Listen to Hebrews 4:16: "Let us then with confidence draw near to the throne of grace, that we may receive mercy and find grace to help in time of need."

How? Doesn't our sin separate us from a holy God? Well, yes. That's why people then never really had confidence to approach him directly even when he invited them. Christians can have this confidence, however, because our sins are forgiven through the perfect sacrifice of Jesus:

> Since we have confidence to enter the holy places by the blood of Jesus,
> by the new and living way that he opened for us through the curtain,
> that is, through his flesh, and since we have a great priest over the
> house of God, let us draw near with a true heart in full assurance of
> faith, with our hearts sprinkled clean from an evil conscience and our
> bodies washed with pure water. (10:19–22)

God's law is in us, not put on us. This happens through the Holy Spirit. While the sacrifice of Jesus clears our past, the Spirit in us assures our future. That's what Jeremiah promised and what Joel echoed.

Those who accept Jesus Christ by faith not only have their past sins forgiven but also receive the Holy Spirit to guide them in following Jesus. Do we always obey the guidance of the Spirit? Unfortunately, no. Even so, he's always there, leading, coaching, and correcting.

Under the old covenant, the law of Moses was like an electric fence. It jolted everyone who crossed the barrier. It was designed to protect through punishment. Under the new covenant, the Spirit inside us is very different. He's more like a compass than like an electric fence. He doesn't limit our movement but frees us by pointing us in the right direction. With the Spirit, it's as though we have a magnetic pull toward righteousness.

Paul stated this reality succinctly in 2 Corinthians 3:6: "The letter kills, but the Spirit gives life." When the Spirit enters us, we receive new hearts. We have no need for a law around us. Our actions are internally motivated.

Key Points

- Jeremiah promised a new covenant during the days of Jerusalem's destruction.

- The hope of a new covenant was common in ancient Israel. Their perpetual sin and punishment showed that the law of Moses wasn't working.

- The new covenant promises three things: personal relationship with the Father, forgiveness of sins through the sacrifice of the Son, and the law of God in our hearts through the Holy Spirit.

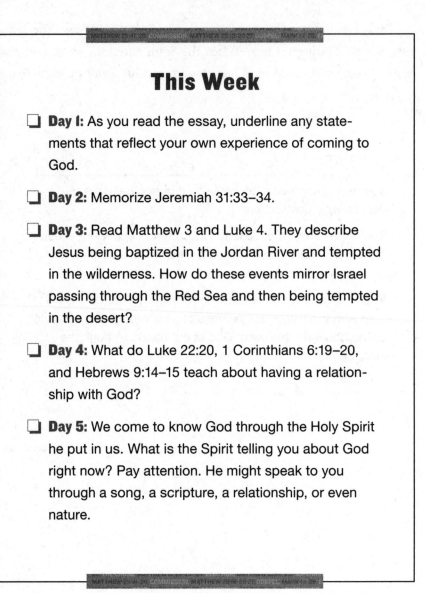

This Week

☐ **Day 1:** As you read the essay, underline any statements that reflect your own experience of coming to God.

☐ **Day 2:** Memorize Jeremiah 31:33–34.

☐ **Day 3:** Read Matthew 3 and Luke 4. They describe Jesus being baptized in the Jordan River and tempted in the wilderness. How do these events mirror Israel passing through the Red Sea and then being tempted in the desert?

☐ **Day 4:** What do Luke 22:20, 1 Corinthians 6:19–20, and Hebrews 9:14–15 teach about having a relationship with God?

☐ **Day 5:** We come to know God through the Holy Spirit he put in us. What is the Spirit telling you about God right now? Pay attention. He might speak to you through a song, a scripture, a relationship, or even nature.

Is Jesus Really God?

Behold, with the clouds of heaven
there came one like a son of man.

—Daniel 7:13

Does it seem a little crazy to you that God would choose to become a human being? I've thought about that a lot. Here's my conclusion: it is crazy. But you know what's crazier? Thinking I could make my way to God. I'm not that good, and I'll *never* be that good!

The problem is obvious. If God hadn't shown himself to us in a way we could understand, how would we have ever known him?

All this is captured in the Bible in a single phrase: *Son of Man.*

The Son of Man

The phrase *son of man* is found 107 times in the Old Testament, and 93 of these are in one book: Ezekiel. God called his prophet "son of man." It's not exactly an insult, but it's not a compliment, either. It reminded Ezekiel of his human frailty.

Psalm 8:4 says, "What is man that you are mindful of him, and the son of man that you care for him?" Again, not an insult, but it certainly puts people in their place. Basically, the term can be friendly, but it's never flattering.

This use is consistent throughout the entire Old Testament, with the single exception of Daniel 7:13. In this unique passage, Daniel had a vision. He saw God ("the Ancient of Days") exalted on his throne (verse 9). Suddenly a divine figure appeared—"one like a son of man" (verse 13)—who was brought into God's presence for a stunning power play: "To him was given dominion and glory and a kingdom, that all peoples, nations, and languages should serve him; his dominion is an everlasting dominion, which shall not pass away, and his kingdom one that shall not be destroyed" (verse 14). How can a mere mortal (a son of man) share God's authority?

When we go to the New Testament, we find yet another odd thing. The term *Son of Man* shows up eighty-five times, almost always in the Gospels. Every use in the Gospels (with the exception of the crowd's question in John 12:34) is not only *about* Jesus but also *spoken by* him. It's as if only Jesus had the boldness to call himself a mere mortal.

With all that in mind, it's safe to assume that only Jesus is the Son of Man. He was virtually the only person to call himself this, and he called himself almost nothing else. But why?

The Big Idea

When we humble ourselves, God exalts us. It's a hard-and-fast rule in Scripture, and Jesus modeled this spiritual law throughout his life.

Son of Man is therefore the perfect title for Jesus. By identifying himself with fragile humans, he gave space for God alone to exalt him. As the apostle Paul said, "God has highly exalted him and bestowed on him the name that is above every name" (Philippians 2:9).

When Caiaphas grilled Jesus at his trial, the high priest demanded an answer: "Are you the Christ, the Son of the Blessed?" (Mark 14:61). The question was a setup. If Jesus said yes, he'd be executed for blasphemy. Jesus responded, "I am, and you will see the *Son of Man* seated at the right hand of Power, and coming with the clouds of heaven" (verse 62). This unique combination of "seated at the right hand of Power" and "coming with the clouds of heaven" is an unmistakable reference to Daniel 7:13–14. Because Jesus knew who he was as God's son, he could live as a human without losing sight of his role at God's right hand.

We can see this odd combination of deity and humanity everywhere in Jesus's ministry. For example, Jesus said, "The Son of Man is lord even of the Sabbath" (Mark 2:28). Think about that for a minute. The Sabbath was established in Eden, so Jesus was claiming the same right as the God who created the world. Jesus also claimed he would judge the world (Matthew 13:41; 16:27). More than that, he claimed the throne in heaven (19:28). This is way bigger than calling dibs on shotgun!

On the other hand, the Son of Man had no place to lay his head (8:20). He came eating and drinking like every other human (11:19). He was betrayed by a friend (26:24, 45) and suffered at the hands of the Sanhedrin (Mark 8:31; 9:12, 31; 10:33; 14:41). He's human in every way—and still claims every right and privilege of God himself.

This reality may seem shocking. Yet how else could God have related to, connected with, and communicated with the human population he loved so desperately? He went to extraordinary lengths to have a relationship with you.

For those who grew up in Christian homes, this idea of God becoming a man may seem normal. For most people, however, this is a crazy idea, especially for Jews and Muslims. If you think about it, they have a point: How could the great God of the universe squeeze himself into the frailty of a human body? But isn't that the point? God can pull off the impossible.

Not only was his incarnation possible, but it's also practical. Jesus's incarnation is a model for us to follow. It's the best route to success at your school, in your family, on your teams, and in your other relationships. When we humble ourselves, God will exalt us. When we live with and for other human beings, God will restore to us our former dignity as caretakers of creation.

Key Points

- In the Old Testament, *son of man* was a title of human weakness.

- Jesus alone is the Son of Man in the New Testament. It was his own title for himself.

- *Son of Man* is the perfect title for Jesus, showing both his full humanity and his full deity.

This Week

❑ **Day 1:** What does this essay teach you about God?

❑ **Day 2:** Memorize Daniel 7:13.

❑ **Day 3:** Read Daniel 3 and 6. How do you see the story of Jesus foreshadowed in the stories of Daniel and his friends?

❑ **Day 4:** How is this idea of God coming to us reflected in Isaiah 9:6, Mark 14:62, and Hebrews 2:6?

❑ **Day 5:** Ask a friend who's not a Christ follower what he or she thinks Jesus would look like if he went to your school.

What Does It Take to Be #Blessed?

> Blessed are you when others revile you and persecute you and utter all kinds of evil against you falsely on my account. Rejoice and be glad, for your reward is great in heaven, for so they persecuted the prophets who were before you.
>
> —MATTHEW 5:11–12

Every six months I do an exercise in my journal called my happiness index. I evaluate six categories of things that make me happy. They cover a range of things from relationships to adrenaline to influence. Your categories would likely differ from mine, but the fact is every human being wants to be happy. There's nothing wrong with that. As we saw in chapter 9, God *wants* you to be happy too.

I created my happiness index because I was going through a difficult season. I needed to take stock of what God was up to in my life. In a sense, the beatitudes, which open Jesus's Sermon on the Mount, are a sort of happiness index with a shocking twist. Each of these eight statements flips our expectations upside down.

Let's take a closer look at how Jesus says, "Fortunate are the unfortunate."

A Sermon of Shockers

The stunning claims of the beatitudes were already scattered throughout Jewish literature. Jesus simply organized them in one shocking stanza. Here they are, along with previous references to the same ideas:

1. *"Blessed are the poor in spirit" (Matthew 5:3).* "It is better to be of a lowly spirit with the poor than to divide the spoil with the proud" (Proverbs 16:19; see also Psalm 34:6; Proverbs 29:23; Isaiah 57:15; 61:1). Isn't it true that those deeply connected to God seem to have peace even if they lack possessions?

2. *"Blessed are those who mourn" (Matthew 5:4).* "Comfort all who mourn" (Isaiah 61:2). Doesn't God often seem closer in times of trouble?

3. *"Blessed are the meek" (Matthew 5:5).* "The meek shall inherit the land" (Psalm 37:11). The humble outlast the proud. (Remember the story of the tortoise and the hare?)

4. *"Blessed are those who hunger and thirst for righteousness" (Matthew 5:6).* "Let justice roll down like waters, and righteousness like an ever-flowing stream" (Amos 5:24; see also 1 Kings 10:9; Job 29:14; Psalm 89:14; Proverbs 29:7; Isaiah 9:7). Isn't right living more satisfying than passing pleasure?

5. *"Blessed are the merciful" (Matthew 5:7).* This statement explains the rabbinic proverb: "So long as you are merciful, He will have mercy on you."[1] Aren't people of mercy often more respected than people of power?

6. *"Blessed are the pure in heart" (Matthew 5:8).* "He who has clean hands and a pure heart . . . will receive blessing from the Lord" (Psalm 24:4–5; see also 73:1; Proverbs 22:11). Isn't a pure heart a reward of its own?

7. *"Blessed are the peacemakers" (Matthew 5:9).* "When a man's ways please the LORD, he makes even his enemies to be at peace with him" (Proverbs 16:7; see also Numbers 25:12; Ezekiel 34:25). The Nobel Prize goes to peacemakers over warriors.

8. *"Blessed are those who are persecuted" (Matthew 5:10).* One of the books written between the Old and New Testaments declares that martyrs (people who are killed for their faith) are blessed by God: "By the blessed death of my brothers, by the eternal destruction of the tyrant, and by the everlasting life of the pious, I will not renounce our noble family ties."[2]

Each beatitude was preceded by a similar statement somewhere in Jewish literature. Yet no one else had ever stacked such countercultural statements in a single manifesto.

The biggest shock came at the end of the passage. Jesus added an explanation for only the final verse, *"Blessed are those who are persecuted."*

Blessed Are the Persecuted

Around the year 165 BC, during the famous Maccabean revolt, a Jewish man named Eleazar was killed for refusing to eat pork (which Jews were not allowed to eat). His courageous words show he believed he would be blessed even if he were persecuted. The historic heroes of the revolt were held in high esteem. They believed they would receive a glorious reward in the afterlife, thus making the persecution worth it.

"Blessed are the persecuted" became a common saying in the centuries between the Testaments. The blessing, however, was specifically for those who suffered for keeping God's law. So, imagine standing in the crowd when Jesus said, "Blessed are you when others revile you and persecute you . . . on my account" (Matthew 5:11). Did Jesus seriously just insert himself where God belonged? Yep. Jesus suggested that true happiness is suffering for him.

We see a similar idea at the sermon's end. Jesus said, "Everyone then who hears these words of mine and does them will be like a wise man who built his house on the rock" (7:24). Jesus was claiming that his words are the foundation for a happy life.

Is it any wonder the crowds stood stunned (verses 28–29)?

Lucky are the unlucky as long as they align themselves with Jesus's words. Christians are part of an upside-down kingdom where losers are winners, the poor are rich, and those who pick up a cross experience resurrection.

Here's the secret: even when life gets hard, if you understand what God is up to on earth, you can still be truly happy.

Key Points

- Jesus changed the measure of happiness, turning the world's values on its head.

- By saying true happiness is found in suffering for him, Jesus implied that he is equal to God.

- Jesus redefined happiness as a relationship with him by living according to his words.

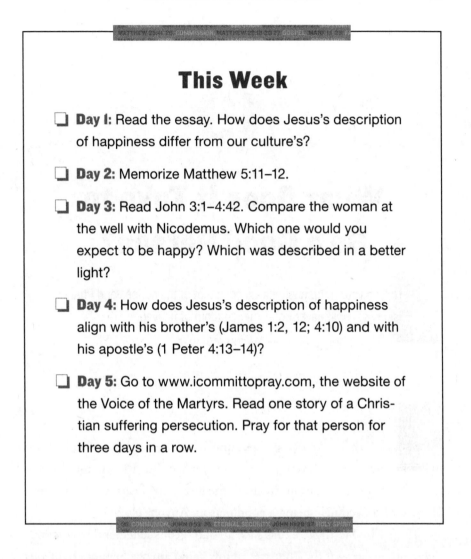

This Week

☐ **Day 1:** Read the essay. How does Jesus's description of happiness differ from our culture's?

☐ **Day 2:** Memorize Matthew 5:11–12.

☐ **Day 3:** Read John 3:1–4:42. Compare the woman at the well with Nicodemus. Which one would you expect to be happy? Which was described in a better light?

☐ **Day 4:** How does Jesus's description of happiness align with his brother's (James 1:2, 12; 4:10) and with his apostle's (1 Peter 4:13–14)?

☐ **Day 5:** Go to www.icommittopray.com, the website of the Voice of the Martyrs. Read one story of a Christian suffering persecution. Pray for that person for three days in a row.

What Does It Take to Be a Good Person?

Unless your righteousness exceeds that of the scribes and Pharisees, you will never enter the kingdom of heaven.

—MATTHEW 5:20

People think I'm good because I have never been drunk, I am polite in public, and I even preach from a stage. But I know me. I know those silent conversations in my head, the lust in my heart, the brokenness of my soul. I need help being a good person. Anyone else?

That's why Matthew 5:20 is such an outrageous statement. Unless your righteousness *exceeds* the Pharisees'? How could anyone be more righteous than the Pharisees? I mean, these religious zealots were like ultramarathoners at a world righteousness race. They fasted twice a week, tithed their garden herbs, and obsessed over hundreds of purity rules.

Is it really possible to exceed the righteousness of the most devoted religious leaders of Jesus's day?

The answer is a resounding yes. Not because we can follow the rules better but because we can improve our motives. Jesus was asking not for a wider righteousness but for one that goes deeper. It's not about simply checking off items like going to church, reading the Bible, or praying. Rather, Jesus calls us to righteous motives. How does this work?

The Practice of Deeper Righteousness

The law can measure actions. But true righteousness grows out of motives. Technically, I keep the law by not killing, but I'm still on the hook if I destroy a life through gossip. If I love my neighbors, it's probably because it's good for me. But if I love my enemies, it's likely because I'm good. Rules can manage only behavior, but Jesus wants to transform our character.

In the last half of Matthew 5, Jesus gave six examples of deeper righteousness. In essence, he said, "The heart of the matter is the heart of the matter." Here are the six and why they matter so much:

1. Murder is against the law. However, murder is merely a symptom. Anger is the motivation behind murder. So Jesus demanded that we deal with anger (verses 21–26). If we don't, we wind up doing more damage through our words than we ever could with a weapon. Far more families are destroyed by gossip than homicide. Far more businesses fail through slander than manslaughter.

2. Adultery may be considered wrong, but lust is generally accepted as inevitable. For Jesus, this was a huge oversight (verses 27–30). Our sex-saturated society has been fueled by lust. We're experiencing unprecedented levels of sexual dysfunction. Never has Jesus's call to personal purity been more important.

3. Divorce was perfectly legal in Judaism. Jesus wanted to put a stop to this family trauma when he said, "Everyone who divorces his wife, except on the ground of sexual immorality, makes her commit adultery, and whoever marries a divorced woman commits adultery" (verse 32). Jesus was pointing out that divorce causes the same damage and exploitation as adultery.

4. Oaths are attempts to distinguish between situations that require honesty and those that don't. Unfortunately, shading or twisting

the truth is fairly normal. Speaking under oath (like laying your hand on a Bible or saying, "Cross my heart") requires a person to be more honest than usual. Jesus pointed out that this is nonsense (verses 33–37). Either we're honest or we're not. Oaths can give a false impression of trustworthiness when we're actually being deceptive. This is serious hypocrisy. Here's a better idea: say what you mean and mean what you say. Or to quote Jesus's brother James, "Let your 'yes' be yes and your 'no' be no" (James 5:12).

5. The law of Moses limited retaliation to equal actions: "An eye for an eye and a tooth for a tooth" (Matthew 5:38; see also Exodus 21:24). Jesus taught a far more effective alternative to retaliation: nonviolent resistance. The idea is simple: Don't just submit to your oppressors, but overcommit to doing them good. That way you'll expose their true motives, and others will see their true colors and come to your defense.

    His famous illustration is to turn the other cheek. Yet look more carefully: "If anyone slaps you on the right cheek, turn to him the other also" (Matthew 5:39). If your attacker (we'll assume he's right handed) gives you a backhanded slap on your right cheek, you expose your left cheek, forcing him to hit you again—only openhanded and with greater force. If others pay attention, they will see the true aggression and violence motivating the attack. Nonviolent resistance is a brilliant strategy proved effective by leaders like Mahatma Gandhi and Martin Luther King Jr.

6. Everyone agrees that we should love our neighbors, our families, and our friends. But Jesus said, "Love your enemies and pray for those who persecute you" (verse 44). For his listeners, this might have been the most offensive thing he said. Remember, Jesus lived in a culture where retaliation was an act of honor. He was talking not about how we feel about our enemies but about how we treat them. Loving an enemy might mean harboring a fugitive, feeding a refugee, or protecting an adversary. This command takes us

back to the seventh beatitude: "Blessed are the peacemakers, for they shall be called sons of God" (verse 9).

But that's not all. To make sure his listeners weren't missing the big idea about how to love their enemies, Jesus raised the bar. He said, "You therefore must be perfect, as your heavenly Father is perfect" (verse 48). First Jesus calls us to be more righteous than the Pharisees; now he expects us to be perfect? That must have gotten people's attention! The word *perfect* here means "mature," not "morally perfect." In short, Jesus was saying we should love as completely, maturely, and openly as God does if we want to do his work in the world. For Jesus, unconditional love is the heart of true righteousness. And that's the way he loved his enemies, even with his dying breath. "Father, forgive them," he prayed, "for they know not what they do" (Luke 23:34).

Key Points

- Jesus calls us to deeper, not wider, righteousness.

- In each of the six illustrations Jesus gave, we're forced to get to the motive behind our action.

- The most difficult command Jesus ever gave was "Love your enemies." Yet he did exactly that through his life and his death on the cross.

This Week

☐ **Day 1:** Read the essay. Which one of Jesus's six illustrations do you need to work on most?

☐ **Day 2:** Memorize Matthew 5:20.

☐ **Day 3:** Samson was a hero of the Old Testament with great physical strength but internal weakness. Read his story in Judges 15–16 in light of Matthew 5:20.

☐ **Day 4:** How do verses 32, 44, and 48 of Matthew 5 explain and expand on what Jesus said in verse 20?

☐ **Day 5:** For the next week, say a prayer every day for someone really difficult to love, specifically your nearest enemy.

How Should I Pray?

Our Father in heaven,
hallowed be your name.
Your kingdom come,
your will be done,
    on earth as it is in heaven.
Give us this day our daily bread,
and forgive us our debts,
    as we also have forgiven our debtors.
And lead us not into temptation,
    but deliver us from evil.

—MATTHEW 6:9–13

I'm a writer and a speaker. Yet my wife will tell you I'm not always good at communication. It's true. I can talk *to* people better than I can talk *with* them. Maybe you've experienced the same thing with social media. It is easier to send a message or post a picture than have an honest, face-to-face conversation.

Likewise, if we want to have a meaningful relationship with God, we need to learn how to talk straight with him. With a little coaching and practice, anyone can get good at prayer. In fact, Jesus provided a model for us. We call it the Lord's Prayer.

"Father": Leverage Your Relationship

By far, the most important lesson on prayer is in the first sentence: "Our Father in heaven, hallowed be your name" (Matthew 6:9). To us, it might seem simple to call God "Father," yet before Jesus, no one ever really did. Jesus, however, almost always opened his prayers with "Father" or the Aramaic equivalent, "Abba."

When we recognize that God in heaven is our caring Father, it changes how we talk with him. I understand that if you have a bad or absent dad, calling God "Father" might be hard for you. However, even those without a father (or with a cruel one) have a deep desire for a good father. It's hardwired into us because that's God's design. Good fathers on earth point to the perfect Father in heaven.

"Kingdom": Embrace God's Agenda

Jesus also taught us to pray, "Your kingdom come, your will be done, on earth as it is in heaven" (verse 10). The power of prayer isn't found in asking God for what you want. Rather, it's in understanding what he wants. When we know God's desires, we can pray for things, and he will say yes. He won't say yes to everything we ask, but he has told us what requests he wants to say yes to.

These include requests for wisdom (James 1:5), the Holy Spirit (Luke 11:13), escape from temptation (Luke 22:40; 1 Corinthians 10:13), and the ability to promote Jesus (Matthew 9:37–38). Let's practice. Seriously. Choose two of those items, and pause right now to ask God for them. Use your own language. Don't try to impress God with words. Just tell him simply and honestly what's in your heart.

When we get these first two areas of prayer right ("Father" and "kingdom"), we can begin to ask God for what we need.

"Give": Ask for What You Need

Jesus promised that when we align ourselves with God's purpose, he will give us everything we need to accomplish everything God wants us to do: "If you ask me anything in my name, I will do it" (John 14:14). God is ready to say yes to your prayers.

To practice this part of prayer, make a wish list for God. Cross off those items that are selfish. Leave on the list those things that would make you a more effective representative of Jesus. Now ask boldly. Next to each item, place the date when you first asked, and leave room to add the date when God answers. (Caution: your list may last for years, and each request may have multiple waves of answers.)

"Forgive": Remove Barriers

Sometimes our prayers don't work because we haven't forgiven someone who has hurt us. Anger, resentment, and bitterness are barriers between God and us as much as between others and us. It doesn't matter whether your hurt was recent or long ago. It doesn't matter whether your anger is justified. That's why Jesus said, "Whenever you stand praying, forgive, if you have anything against anyone, so that your Father also who is in heaven may forgive you your trespasses" (Mark 11:25).

Forgiving others frees us to have an open relationship with God. When we forgive others as God forgave us, our prayers will flow more freely and be answered more readily. Consider for a moment whether there's a person (dead or alive) with whom you're at odds. Just speak that person's name before God, and ask for the strength to forgive. If you can't yet forgive, ask for the desire to do so.

"Deliver": Follow a Guide

Sin is another barrier to answered prayers. When we're behaving in ways that dishonor God and disgrace our human dignity, it's hard for us to have open communication with him.

To pray for deliverance from sin, simply tell God what he already knows. Confess out loud one or two habits or activities you're not so proud of. Genuinely apologize, and ask God to give you strength to resist temptation. This is not a time to beat yourself up. Jesus's death on the cross saved you from this sin. But if you don't confess, it will weigh you down.

God removes sin from our lives when we confess it to him and make things right wherever possible. The Bible calls this repentance, and it comes with a promise of forgiveness: "If we confess our sins, he is faithful and just to forgive us our sins and to cleanse us from all unrighteousness" (1 John 1:9). This point takes us full circle to the fatherhood of God. He doesn't want you isolated from others or separated from him. That's why we can pray boldly even if our behavior is off track.

Key Points

- The most important lesson on prayer is to recognize God as Father.

- When our prayers are aligned with God's agenda, our requests are approved in his time.

- Our prayers are hindered when we withhold forgiveness from others and continue sinful habits.

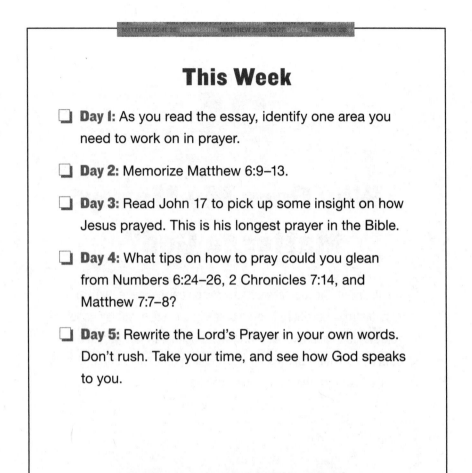

This Week

☐ **Day 1:** As you read the essay, identify one area you need to work on in prayer.

☐ **Day 2:** Memorize Matthew 6:9–13.

☐ **Day 3:** Read John 17 to pick up some insight on how Jesus prayed. This is his longest prayer in the Bible.

☐ **Day 4:** What tips on how to pray could you glean from Numbers 6:24–26, 2 Chronicles 7:14, and Matthew 7:7–8?

☐ **Day 5:** Rewrite the Lord's Prayer in your own words. Don't rush. Take your time, and see how God speaks to you.

21

Why Does My Money Matter to God?

> Do not lay up for yourselves treasures on earth, where moth and rust destroy and where thieves break in and steal, but lay up for yourselves treasures in heaven, where neither moth nor rust destroys and where thieves do not break in and steal. For where your treasure is, there your heart will be also.
>
> —MATTHEW 6:19–21

Whether you get money from a job or your parents, your money is spiritual. Seriously, it is. More than 2,300 verses in the Bible speak about money. Only five hundred speak about prayer. Even fewer address faith. Why? Because God knows that what we do with our money, even how we think about it, tells the truth about our hearts. There's a direct connection between our wallets and our faith.

God Wants Our Hearts, Not Our Money

Jesus said, "Where your treasure is, there your heart will be also" (Matthew 6:21). Many people think our money follows our hearts. The idea is that we give to things we care about. That's sometimes true. But it's always true that our hearts follow our money.

The way we manage money reveals whether "in God we trust." After all, God owns everything. Psalm 24:1 says, "The earth is the LORD's and the fullness thereof, the world and those who dwell therein." Your phone, room, job, and anything else you'd call yours are actually God's. Your college fund, car, and clothes are in the same category as the Milky Way, ring-tailed lemurs, and the Grand Canyon—all his. If God is the creator, he's also the owner.

What does that make you? Just a manager (called a steward in the Bible). Which actually takes the pressure off, while at the same time piling on responsibility. Our job with stuff is to steward, not seize.

If money is your master, God cannot be. This is Jesus's idea, not mine: "No one can serve two masters, for either he will hate the one and love the other, or he will be devoted to the one and despise the other. You cannot serve God and money" (Matthew 6:24).

Stewardship Is Spiritual

It's difficult to see money as spiritual. Church, prayer, and the Bible are in one category. Clothes, shoes, and music are in another one. But that's not how God sees things. Whether we realize it or not, how we manage money affects our spiritual lives. It can hinder or accelerate prayer. It can replace or promote worship. It can drive us toward or away from the church. It can blind us to God's Word or open windows to wisdom.

From God's perspective, our money is an eternal resource. Though we can't take it with us, we can send it on ahead. Jesus said as much: "Do not lay up for yourselves treasures on earth, where moth and rust destroy and where thieves break in and steal, but lay up for yourselves treasures in heaven, where neither moth nor rust destroys and where thieves do not break in and steal" (Matthew 6:19–20). Because of this truth, we need to treat our finances as kingdom-building resources.

Paul said in Colossians 3:5, "Put to death therefore what is earthly in you: sexual immorality, impurity, passion, evil desire, and covetousness, which is idolatry." Our lust for possessions and security is the single greatest hindrance to fully following Jesus. Whatever we own ultimately owns us.

Generosity Brings Blessing

Typically we focus on generosity as a blessing to those who receive it. God focuses on the blessing that generosity offers to the giver.

We have Paul to thank for a quote from Jesus in Acts 20:35 (which is the only known saying of Jesus that wasn't recorded in the Gospels): "It is more blessed to give than to receive." We all know this is true. Even around the tree on Christmas morning, our greatest joy comes when others are unwrapping gifts we've given them.

Not only does giving bless us, but it also opens the floodgates of God's blessing on our lives. It's as if God gives us wealth so we can give it away. Then he eagerly awaits our emptied hands to pour out more. The more we give God's resources to build God's kingdom, the more he funnels in our direction. As wise King Solomon said, "Honor the Lord with your wealth and with the firstfruits of all your produce; then your barns will be filled with plenty, and your vats will be bursting with wine" (Proverbs 3:9–10). Jesus paraphrased the principle with this famous quote: "Give, and it will be given to you. Good measure, pressed down, shaken together, running over, will be put into your lap. For with the measure you use it will be measured back to you" (Luke 6:38). Hence the old saying "You cannot outgive God."

The Bible outlines this kind of redistribution under two concepts: tithes and offerings.

A tithe is the first 10 percent of all earnings. When we give that to God, it affirms (and reminds us of) his ownership of the other 90 percent. Don't make the mistake of giving your last 10 percent. That's merely a tip that says, "Thank you." A tithe is the first 10 percent that says to God, "I submit to you as owner of it all."

Offerings are what you choose to give in other ways. These could be handouts to the helpless, contributions to Christian or other charitable organizations, or personal gifts to bless individuals you care about. Generosity is an offering that exceeds the tithe. This is where the full joy of generosity lives. Paul said, "God loves a cheerful giver" (2 Corinthians 9:7). Cheerfulness tends to be the result of giving, not the cause. Jesus taught this principle this way: "Where your treasure is, there your heart will be also" (Matthew 6:21).

Key Points

- God wants your heart, not your money.
- Stewardship is spiritual. We are managing what God owns.
- Generosity blesses the generous.

This Week

☐ **Day 1:** Based on this essay, what do you need to do differently with your money?

☐ **Day 2:** Memorize Matthew 6:19–21.

☐ **Day 3:** Read Joshua 5:13–7:26. What does this story show about how God views greed?

☐ **Day 4:** Write one principle about money from each of these passages: Matthew 19:16–30, Acts 20:35, and Philippians 4:13.

☐ **Day 5:** Sit down with a parent, coach, or other mentor, and write out a budget that includes a 10 percent tithe to your local church.

What Is Right Religion?

Whatever you wish that others would do to you, do also to them,
for this is the Law and the Prophets.

—MATTHEW 7:12

Several years ago I memorized the entire Sermon on the Mount
(Matthew 5–7). I tried hard to live out each verse I memorized for at least
one day. For me, the hardest to put into practice *by far* was this week's core
text. We call it the Golden Rule. It is the essence of right religion. Sure, it
fits in a tweet, yet it demands your entire life.

Pure and Undefiled Religion

James, Jesus's half brother, wrote a book of the Bible called—you guessed
it—James. He explained how to apply parts of the Sermon on the Mount.
For example, in James 1:27 he taught how to apply the Golden Rule. Let's
read the verse and connect the dots: "Religion that is pure and undefiled
before God the Father is this: to visit orphans and widows in their afflic-
tion, and to keep oneself unstained from the world."

The purpose of religion is not merely to avoid bad stuff. Pure religion
(as James called it) is first to serve people, especially the most helpless. Does

this mean that personal morality doesn't matter? Of course not. It's just that when our main goal in life is to not sin, we tend to forget the people who need God the most. But when serving the least of these becomes a major way we express our love for God, pursuing love replaces avoiding sin. We purposely enter the places and relationships where his love is most needed. The truly religious become his ambassadors.

What about our personal morality, then? Serving others actually grows it! We live by a higher standard when other people are spiritually dependent on us. More responsibility always leads to more personal growth than just trying to increase our own self-control.

Let's be clear: neither Jesus nor James was replacing ethics with social service. The biblical word *righteousness* implies both. So, how do we pursue holiness *and* serve others? Many assume that going to church, reading the Bible, and praying will lead to a life that honors God. Too often those practices lead to someone being "holier than thou." The Bible is clear: serve others—truly serve them—and you'll see your personal holiness improve as well.

What Does the Lord Require of You?

Both Jesus and James built their teaching on the prophetic tradition of Israel. Here are several examples. The prophet Micah said, "He has told you, O man, what is good; and what does the LORD require of you but to do justice, and to love kindness, and to walk humbly with your God?" (6:8). This famous Old Testament statement tells us what God *really* wants.

The bottom line throughout Scripture is this: the right actions with the wrong heart are offensive to God. Why? Because when we go to church, say our prayers, and perform our religious duties without the right heart, we treat God like a vending machine—"Give me; give me; give me." Our sacrifice becomes a bribe to God instead of a blessing to his people.

We see this principle when the prophet Samuel told King Saul, "To obey is better than sacrifice" (1 Samuel 15:22). King David sang a song about it: "In sacrifice and offering you have not delighted. . . . Burnt offering and sin offering you have not required" (Psalm 40:6). This psalm is quoted in Hebrews 10:5–6. It's a big deal!

David's son Solomon wrote, "To do righteousness and justice is more acceptable to the LORD than sacrifice" (Proverbs 21:3). But probably the most similar passage to Micah's is from his contemporary, the prophet Isaiah. These are words you *don't* want to hear God say!

> What to me is the multitude of your sacrifices?
>> says the LORD;
> I have had enough of burnt offerings of rams
>> and the fat of well-fed beasts;
> I do not delight in the blood of bulls,
>> or of lambs, or of goats.

> When you come to appear before me,
>> who has required of you
>> this trampling of my courts?
> Bring no more vain offerings;
>> incense is an abomination to me. . . .
> Remove the evil of your deeds from before my eyes;
> cease to do evil,
>> learn to do good;
> seek justice,
>> correct oppression;
> bring justice to the fatherless,
>> plead the widow's cause. (1:11–13, 16–17)

The passage brings us right back to Micah 6:8. What does the Lord require of us?

1. *Do justice.* The phrase literally means "to make justice." We use our influence and resources to stand up for those who cannot stand up for themselves.
2. *Love kindness.* This word *kindness* is one of the weightier words in the Old Testament. It implies the covenant loyalty of God. We

would use it today in relation to marriage, adoption, or even a last
will and testament. To love kindness means more than being
nice. It means absolute allegiance to God.

3. *Walk humbly with our God.* Why does our relationship with God
take humility? Because pride blinds us. We think we're religious
because of our behavior, but he knows our motives.

Think about this: How does God view our religious activities? Are they
sacrifices or bribes? The quickest way to tell is to see whether our religious
deeds improve the plight of the poor in our communities. If the church
doesn't care for those God cares for, then what good are we really doing?

Key Points

- When James spoke of religion as care for widows and
  orphans, he showed how his perspective matched that of his
  half brother Jesus.

- As Christians, we should both serve others and pursue
  holiness.

- James, like the Old Testament prophets, calls us to justice,
  kindness, and humility as true religious expression.

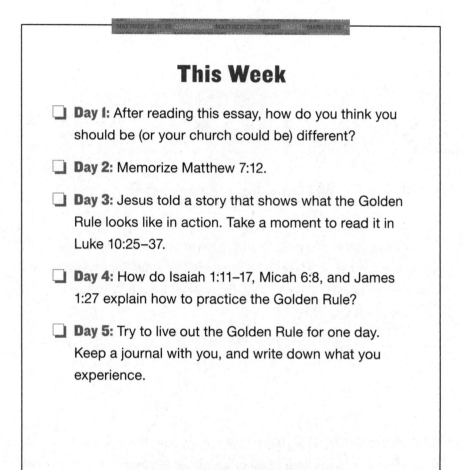

This Week

☐ **Day 1:** After reading this essay, how do you think you should be (or your church could be) different?

☐ **Day 2:** Memorize Matthew 7:12.

☐ **Day 3:** Jesus told a story that shows what the Golden Rule looks like in action. Take a moment to read it in Luke 10:25–37.

☐ **Day 4:** How do Isaiah 1:11–17, Micah 6:8, and James 1:27 explain how to practice the Golden Rule?

☐ **Day 5:** Try to live out the Golden Rule for one day. Keep a journal with you, and write down what you experience.

Who Is Jesus?

Jesus told his disciples, "If anyone would come after me, let him deny himself and take up his cross and follow me. For whoever would save his life will lose it, but whoever loses his life for my sake will find it."

—MATTHEW 16:24–25

After my parents' divorce, my brothers and I had to decide whether we would live with Mom or with Dad. My father was a Christian, my mother rejected Jesus, and I loved them both with all my heart. Even though I was just twelve at the time, I understood that my real decision was not whom to live with. My real decision was who I believed Jesus was. Looking back, I can see that my choice to live with Dad shaped nearly every decision I made afterward.

One day Jesus put a question to his apostles that would change everything for them too. He asked, "Who do you say that I am?" (Matthew 16:15).

The Confession

In the middle of his three-year ministry, Jesus took off with his apostles for a pivotal experience. They hiked to the northernmost border of Israel near Caesarea Philippi. At a certain point, Jesus turned to his followers and asked them to tell him who they thought he was. Peter answered for the whole group: Jesus is the Messiah—"the Christ, the Son of the living God" (verse 16). This long-awaited confession was anticipated in the opening chapters of all four gospels (Matthew 1:1; 2:4; Mark 1:1; Luke 1:31–35; 2:11; John 1:17, 49).

This was a monumental moment. Jesus not only affirmed Peter's confession but explained what it actually meant (Mark 8:31–32). They expected that the Christ would be a king who would conquer their enemies. What they got was a Savior who would die for their sins. Jesus would not kill his enemies but die for them!

The Objection

When Jesus told them his destiny was death, Peter refused to believe his words. He exclaimed, "Far be it from you, Lord! This shall never happen to you" (Matthew 16:22). The original Greek wording is stronger than our English translation. You could read it something like "When hell freezes over!" (which you might expect from a fisherman like Peter). But Jesus's response is even stronger, possibly his harshest words ever: "Get behind me, Satan!" (verse 23). He just called his right-hand man the devil. Why?

Jesus was harsh but not unfair. Satan had tempted Jesus in the desert in exactly the same way (Matthew 4:1–11; Luke 4:1–13). The devil tried to derail Jesus's mission by tempting him to use his power and prestige to avoid the Cross. Satan (and Peter) urged Jesus to claim his God status to avoid the human experience of pain and suffering.

The Call

Jesus followed his rebuke of Peter with what would become his most frequently cited saying in the Gospels: "If anyone would come after me, let him deny himself and take up his cross and follow me. For whoever would save his life will lose it, but whoever loses his life for my sake will find it" (Matthew 16:24–25).

Jesus was talking no longer about his own death but about that of his disciples. He commanded his followers to take up their own crosses. Paul also identified discipleship as cross-bearing. For example, "I have been crucified with Christ. It is no longer I who live, but Christ who lives in me. And the life I now live in the flesh I live by faith in the Son of God, who loved me and gave himself for me" (Galatians 2:20). The cross isn't merely what Jesus did for us; it's what he modeled for us. Being a disciple is not just receiving what Jesus did; it's imitating him—living *how he lived.*

Jesus's death saved our souls. We sing this truth at church, and we hear it from pulpits. We thank God for his grace in sending his son to save us for eternity. Clear enough. So, what's the purpose of our crosses? Jesus said if we don't take up a cross, we're unable to truly follow him (Matthew 10:38). We must live as the walking dead of sorts. Only then will we conquer our sinful passions.

The purpose of cross-bearing is not simply self-denial. It's so much more. Our sacrifice isn't to make better versions of us. Like Jesus's death, our suffering and sacrifice make a better version of *society as a whole.* Jesus died to pay the penalty for people's personal sins. Likewise, we die to ourselves—ego, selfishness, greed—to reverse the effects of sin in society, families, and communities.

If we got serious about this kind of sacrifice, we'd see incredible results. The church could eliminate the foster-care system. If the church were to focus medical attention on malaria, we could effectively eliminate one of the single greatest causes of death in human history. And those are just two examples. Only in the church is there a realistic hope of eradicating racism. Only in Christ have Jew and Greek, slave and free, male and female been united in fellowship and purpose (Galatians 3:28). The list could go on, and it's long.

We know the church could do this because we've seen it happen before. Beginning with the first-century church, the greatest steps forward in culture, art, medicine, compassion, education, poverty relief, and the protection of women, children, and the marginalized have come primarily from those who follow Jesus with crosses strapped to their backs.

This point brings us back to our original question: Who do you say Jesus is? If we believe he's merely a prophet from the past, a hero of our faith, we have missed the purpose of the Messiah. Suffering and sacrifice are his greatest achievements. As his disciple, they will be yours as well.

If we confess him as Lord, we're obligated to follow his example. We cannot celebrate a Lord we won't imitate.

Key Points

- The most important question you will ever answer is "Who is Jesus?"

- To be our Savior, Jesus had to suffer.

- Just as Jesus died on a cross so we could be saved, we take up our crosses so society can be saved.

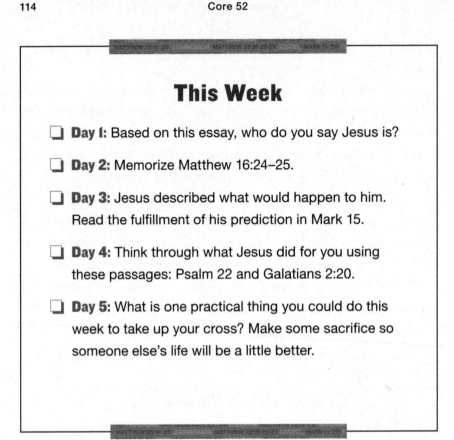

This Week

☐ **Day 1:** Based on this essay, who do you say Jesus is?

☐ **Day 2:** Memorize Matthew 16:24–25.

☐ **Day 3:** Jesus described what would happen to him. Read the fulfillment of his prediction in Mark 15.

☐ **Day 4:** Think through what Jesus did for you using these passages: Psalm 22 and Galatians 2:20.

☐ **Day 5:** What is one practical thing you could do this week to take up your cross? Make some sacrifice so someone else's life will be a little better.

Does God Want Me?

Many are called, but few are chosen.
—MATTHEW 22:14

Elementary school recess is hard for boys who are small for their age like I was. I was never picked first for kickball. In fact, I wasn't picked in the first half of the class . . . and that included many of the girls! Trust me when I say that being chosen is a big deal. So, imagine what a shock and joy it was for me to learn that God wanted me on his team.

This week we will listen to a surprising story Jesus told (Matthew 22:2–13). It helps answer the question "Does God want me?" See whether you can find yourself in his story.

The Parable

Once upon a time, a king threw a banquet celebrating his son's wedding. All who were invited refused to come, and some of them shamelessly abused and even murdered the very messengers inviting them.

The king, of course, was furious and destroyed his enemies. Yet the wedding hall was still empty. So he sent other servants to invite anyone they could find—outcast, downcast, and dirty—those you would never ever think *could be invited*. They came in droves.

Here's the story's summary: "Many are called, but few are chosen" (verse 14).

This word *chosen* could be translated as "elected." Jesus's parable explains the basic process of election: they were invited and they came. It's that simple. Many prominent people were invited but refused to come. They were not elected. Others didn't deserve an invitation but received one and came gladly. They were elected.

The Principle

At the risk of oversimplifying, we can point out two basic views of election: (1) God alone chooses who goes to heaven and who does not, and (2) God alone chooses the requirements for salvation, and we get to choose whether or not to enter.

Very smart (and good) people disagree on the definition of *election*—and for good reasons. With all due respect to other views, we'll start with Jesus's own definition of *election* as drawn from the above parable: God sets the rules for the party and sends out the invitations. We choose whether or not to accept.

Let's clarify a few important points:

- *Everyone is invited.* The rich and poor of the parable all got an invite. Some in Jesus's audience were the put-together religious type. Others were farmers, day laborers, or outcasts whose daily means of survival might make them "unclean." From the top of society to the bottom, all were invited.

  This principle is spelled out in 2 Peter 3:9: "The Lord is not slow to fulfill his promise as some count slowness, but is patient toward you, not wishing that any should perish, but that all should reach repentance." According to Scripture, God "desires all people to be saved" (1 Timothy 2:4).

- *Not everyone gets the same invitation.* God is inclusive, but the reality is that those of us born in the West have more opportunity to hear the gospel and respond freely than those born in other parts of the world or other periods in history. Does that fact mean God isn't fair? Yes, that's exactly what it means. God isn't fair. He is, however, gracious to all.
- *You must respond to the invitation.* Election is not just the invitation. It's a particular response to the invitation. God alone invites. Humans, however, under God's sovereignty, have to respond.

  Jesus himself taught, "Strive to enter through the narrow door" (Luke 13:24). It's on us to respond to the invitation.
- *God knows who will respond.* God doesn't force your hand, but he does see in advance how you'll play it. In other words, he *knows* what you'll do before you ever do it.

  Every parent with small children has had a similar experience. A mom or dad watching a kiddo pretty much knows when the child is about to jump, touch something, or cry. It's the same with God. Except he sees further out.

  God determines the boundaries of salvation. He sees who will respond and who will not. His call is to all; his election is for those he sees will step inside his predetermined boundaries of salvation.

  Paul summarized it this way:

Those whom he foreknew he also predestined to be conformed to the image of his Son, in order that he might be the firstborn among many brothers. And those whom he predestined he also called, and those whom he called he also justified, and those whom he justified he also glorified. (Romans 8:29–30)

The Purpose

So, what do we do with individual predestination?[1] Both the Old and the New Testaments highlight individuals whom God elected and predestined. The list is long:

- Abraham (Nehemiah 9:7)
- Jacob (Genesis 25:19–34; 27:1–41; Malachi 1:2–3; Romans 9:10–13)
- Pharaoh (Exodus 9:16; Romans 9:17)
- David (1 Samuel 16:1–13)
- Josiah (1 Kings 13:1–3)
- Cyrus (2 Chronicles 36:22–23; Isaiah 41:25; 44:28; 45:1–13)
- Jeremiah (Jeremiah 1:5)
- John the Baptist (Isaiah 40:3; Malachi 4:5–6; Luke 1:17)
- Jesus (Isaiah 42:1; Matthew 12:18; Luke 9:35; Acts 2:23; 4:28)
- Judas Iscariot (Psalm 41:9; 69:25; 109:8; Mark 14:10; Acts 1:20)
- The twelve apostles (Luke 6:13; John 6:70; 15:16)
- Paul (Acts 9:15; 13:2; Romans 1:1; Galatians 1:15–16; Ephesians 3:7)
- Rufus (Romans 16:13)

Don't miss this truth! God ordains individuals to a task, not a destiny. Abraham was called to found a nation, and Pharaoh to release that nation. David was chosen to lead a kingdom, and Cyrus to restore that kingdom after captivity. John was destined to prepare for Jesus's coming, and Jesus to die on a cross.

If God calls you to a task, you will perform that task—either his way or yours. Regardless, you will do what God calls you to do.

Key Points

- According to Jesus, election is God's invitation plus a person's response.

- God sets the boundary of salvation and sees beforehand who will enter in.

- Individuals are predestined to a task, not a destiny.

This Week

☐ **Day 1:** As you read the essay, jot down a couple of truths that remind you that God chose you.

☐ **Day 2:** Memorize Matthew 22:14.

☐ **Day 3:** Some people think they are too bad for God to want. Read Acts 9:1–31. It is the story of a notorious persecutor of the church who would become one of its greatest leaders.

☐ **Day 4:** In Joshua 24:15, Romans 8:29–30, and 2 Peter 3:9, what does the Bible say about God choosing you?

☐ **Day 5:** Based on your skills, talents, and abilities, identify one task *you* are uniquely shaped to do for Jesus—not twenty years from now but this week. Grab a friend for accountability and make it happen.

Is the Supernatural World Actually Real?

He will say to those on his left, "Depart from me, you cursed,
into the eternal fire prepared for the devil and his angels."

—MATTHEW 25:41

Have you ever encountered an angel or maybe a demon? I have.
Since I don't want to freak you out, I won't tell you the details, but I do
believe that the spiritual realm is real. Jesus definitely thought so too and
taught as much. In fact, look closely and you'll realize that his statement
above includes all facets of the supernatural world: hell, demons, angels.

This essay is a simple survey with a single point—to raise your awareness that you're not alone in this world. An unseen reality is raging all
around us.

Fast Facts on Hell

According to Scripture, hell is a real place of torment. It's described with
the metaphors of flames, sulfur, worms (don't want to even think about
that one!), darkness, and gnashing of teeth (Isaiah 66:24; Matthew 22:13;

25:41; Mark 9:48; 2 Thessalonians 1:8–9; Revelation 14:11; 20:10). Because these passages describe future and spiritual realities, it's difficult to know how literally to take those details.

What we know for sure is that hell (or, more accurately, the lake of fire) is the place of eternal punishment for our sins on earth. This punishment may seem extreme. But maybe that's because we fail to see sin from God's perspective: as rebellion against perfect holiness.

Technically, God doesn't throw people into hell. (Remember last week's essay? *God wants you!*) Individuals reject his presence. Where else are they to go, then, but to a place inhabited by others who refuse God's authority? And let's be honest: people who reject God on this earth have made their own hell here. Perhaps the descriptions of hell in the Bible are not so much God's design for "bad people." Maybe they are descriptions of what unbelievers create *for themselves,* apart from the control of the Holy Spirit.

Fast Facts on Demons

Demons are spirits who rebelled against God, their creator. They are real, and they're no joke. They know who Jesus is (Mark 1:24, 34) and believe in God (James 2:19), yet they choose to follow Satan, who is himself a fallen angel (Revelation 12:7–9). They seek to inhabit human beings (Matthew 12:43). Yet they're naturally destructive, causing blindness (Matthew 12:22), deafness and muteness (Mark 9:25), deformity (Luke 13:11), seizures (Matthew 17:14–18), mental illness (Matthew 11:18; Luke 7:33; John 7:20; 8:48, 52; 10:20, 21), and suicidal impulses (Matthew 17:15; Mark 5:5). They tend to be loud (Mark 1:26) and are organized into a global army (Revelation 16:14). While they wield considerable power, they'll ultimately be destroyed (Revelation 20:1–10). Though they can perform some miracles (Revelation 16:14), their power is limited by God (Romans 8:38–39; Revelation 9:20).

Demons tend to get a foothold in a human soul through four channels: cultic activities (such as séances) and the classic trio of sex, drugs, and any musical style that honors the dark spiritual world. Participating in these does not guarantee that a demon will gain access to you. They are, however, the most common conduits.

For most of us, three quick steps will minimize demonic influence: Scripture (reading or quoting aloud), worship music, and praying out loud in Jesus's name. These three activities drive demons crazy. You can actually irritate them away (just like your little brother does to you). Doing so won't keep them away permanently, but it will offer a reprieve. The stronger the hold of a demon, the more extreme the measures needed to repel it. (A helpful resource is Neil Anderson's *The Bondage Breaker*.)

This point takes us to Ephesians 6:12: "We do not wrestle against flesh and blood, but against the rulers, against the authorities, against the cosmic powers over this present darkness, against the spiritual forces of evil in the heavenly places." Paul went on to list the armor of God we have as Christians (verses 13–18). The only offensive weapon Paul mentioned is "the sword of the Spirit, which is the word of God" (verse 17).

Fast Facts on Angels

Angels are spiritual beings who serve God. The Greek word *aggelos* actually means "messenger." Notice how angels hover around the coming of Jesus, whether it's his first coming or his final coming.

They also minister to Jesus (Mark 1:13) and to his people (Psalm 91:11–12). They comforted Jesus in Gethsemane (Luke 22:43), carried Lazarus to Abraham's side (16:22), and released the apostles from prison (Acts 5:19; 12:7–11). An angel led Philip to the Ethiopian eunuch (8:26); another assassinated Herod Agrippa (12:23); still another predicted Paul's safe arrival in Rome (27:23–24). In fact, Hebrews 1:14 says, "Are they not all ministering spirits sent out to serve for the sake of those who are to inherit salvation?" That's why they celebrate whenever a sinner repents (Luke 15:10). In short, angels announce and assist.

Key Points

- Hell is a horrible place described in the Bible with the best metaphors available.

- Demons gain greater access through the occult, sex, drugs, and dark music. They are repelled through Scripture, praise, and prayer, especially when we sing or speak aloud.

- Angels announced Jesus's arrival on the earth, and they assist believers in carrying out their call.

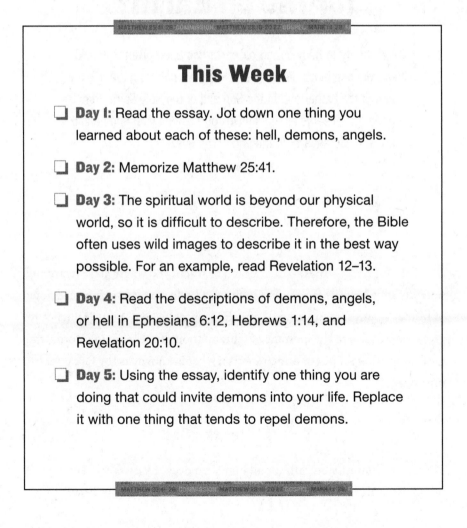

This Week

☐ **Day 1:** Read the essay. Jot down one thing you learned about each of these: hell, demons, angels.

☐ **Day 2:** Memorize Matthew 25:41.

☐ **Day 3:** The spiritual world is beyond our physical world, so it is difficult to describe. Therefore, the Bible often uses wild images to describe it in the best way possible. For an example, read Revelation 12–13.

☐ **Day 4:** Read the descriptions of demons, angels, or hell in Ephesians 6:12, Hebrews 1:14, and Revelation 20:10.

☐ **Day 5:** Using the essay, identify one thing you are doing that could invite demons into your life. Replace it with one thing that tends to repel demons.

What Is God's Purpose for Me on Earth?

All authority in heaven and on earth has been given to me. Go therefore and make disciples of all nations, baptizing them in the name of the Father and of the Son and of the Holy Spirit, teaching them to observe all that I have commanded you. And behold, I am with you always, to the end of the age.

—MATTHEW 28:18–20

If you've ever heard me preach or teach, you might have heard me say, "Let's make Jesus famous." It may sound odd, since *Jesus* is already one of history's best-known names. I am challenging us to use our influence to give others access to the message of Christ. Though these are my words, the idea comes straight out of our core verse, what is known as the Great Commission.

The "All" of the Call

The Great Commission calls for all hands on deck. Every Christian, young or old, is on the team, expanding God's global kingdom. But how?

Sharing our faith can be intimidating. What if I mess up or someone calls me a hypocrite? What if I lose a friend? What if I lose a scholarship? These are all valid questions that Jesus dealt with in the commission.

"All authority in heaven and on earth has been given to me" (Matthew 28:18). Because of Jesus's perfect life, sacrificial death, and victorious resurrection, God made him ruler and judge of the world. When we enter Jesus's service, we go with his authority. That's what Paul meant when he called us ambassadors: "We are ambassadors for Christ, God making his appeal through us. We implore you on behalf of Christ, be reconciled to God" (2 Corinthians 5:20). This is crazy! We actually have the authority to offer forgiveness on Jesus's behalf.

Let's be clear: Jesus's approved method of salvation is grace through faith. In other words, we cannot offer forgiveness to anyone who hasn't pledged allegiance to Jesus. But don't miss the magnitude of this authority. We offer God's grace through Jesus's blood. This is not a job reserved for a priest or bishop but the right and responsibility of every Christ follower.

A lot of people worry about someone asking a question they can't answer. Jesus knew that might happen. Here is his solution: "When they deliver you over, do not be anxious how you are to speak or what you are to say, for what you are to say will be given to you in that hour. For it is not you who speak, but the Spirit of your Father speaking through you" (Matthew 10:19–20).

"Make disciples of all nations" (28:19). One of the most extraordinary things about Jesus is his global goals. Even at the earliest stages, Jesus's ministry was always outward focused. His healings, preaching, and commands always push us further out toward people who are less like us.

This outward focus is the opposite of almost every other religious tradition. Other traditions drive followers further inward. Islam, Judaism, Buddhism, and others call people to deeper devotion, more demanding rituals, or higher knowledge. But for Christians, it's our evangelism and social service that fulfill our deepest commitments to Christ Jesus.

"Teaching them to observe all that I have commanded you" (verse 20).

This task seems impossible, right? Who can remember, let alone obey, all the commands of Jesus?

Well, they're not that hard to remember, since Jesus reduced all the commands of the Old Testament to two simple instructions: love God and love people (22:37–40). While those commands are easy to memorize, they're impossible to perfect. That's why they require teaching. The job of every Christian is to help apply these commands. Teaching is the role of parents with their children, coaches with their players, and older students with younger students. (The fact that you're reading this book means you have something to share!)

Wherever God places you, your purpose is clear: to help at least one person take at least one step toward God and others.

In case we think this is too much to ask, Jesus added a promise at the end: "Behold, I am with you always, to the end of the age" (28:20). Because this is God's mission and—since we're working alongside him—our co-mission, he's fully prepared to be fully present. Jesus himself will continue to be with us through the Holy Spirit. He will guide us, correct us, and provide the wisdom, power, and opportunities we need.

When the commission is completed, we will welcome a new age of eternity. We will see Jesus face to face. All our earthly troubles will be no more!

Make Disciples

Defined in a single sentence, a disciple is a learner or student. However, discipleship is less about learning information and more about experiencing life transformation. It's not about knowing the most *about* Jesus or the Bible. It's about being changed to live and love *like Jesus would*. You can see why the call to "make disciples of all nations" is at the heart of the Great Commission and is the life purpose of every Christ follower.

From the moment we drip-dry in the baptistery until we cross the threshold of eternity, our calling is to partner with God to make Jesus famous.

Key Points

- The Great Commission is universal: reach all people in all places at all times.

- It is God's mission and our co-mission.

- We make disciples by making Jesus famous and mentoring others in loyalty to him.

This Week

☐ **Day 1:** What does this essay tell you about your life purpose?

☐ **Day 2:** Memorize Matthew 28:18–20.

☐ **Day 3:** The first non-Jewish person to accept the gospel was a man named Cornelius. Read his story in Acts 10–11 to see how the Great Commission finally broke all cultural and ethnic barriers.

☐ **Day 4:** What do Mark 16:15–16, John 20:21–23, and 2 Corinthians 5:20 tell you about our responsibility in God's mission?

☐ **Day 5:** Think of one person whom you could bring at least one step closer to Jesus. For the next week, set a daily alarm on your phone to remind you to pray for that person. Ask God to show you what to do.

27

Why Is Christianity Good News?

The beginning of the gospel of Jesus Christ, the Son of God.

—MARK 1:1

Stephanie was the first person I ever remember baptizing into Jesus. I had grown up in the church, but she had never really heard the gospel. I'll never forget her excitement—or my surprise—when I told her about Jesus. She taught me that the gospel, which is often taken for granted by church kids, really is a life-changing message.

The word *gospel* literally means "good news." You see, the story of Jesus's life, death, and resurrection is incredibly good news for those who realize they are lost.

The Gospel and Politics

In every major city across the ancient Roman world, there were messengers bringing good news from the capital. (What—no Twitter?) The gospel of these Roman heralds was usually big news about the highest leader of the land—when the emperor got married, let's say, or had a baby, or when one of his generals won an important battle. In each case, officials spread the good news to all parts of the empire.

The messages were inscribed on parchment, stones, and pillars so the people could celebrate and rally around their ruler. That's an important sentence. In fact, read that last part again: so the people could celebrate and rally around their ruler!

Christians used *gospel* for exactly the same reason. They wanted to exalt their ruler, Jesus, who was the source of their spiritual prosperity. Christians made this claim in direct opposition to the Roman emperor's claim to be the ruler of the world. By the very use of the term, they were telling a different story: The emperor of Rome was not the ruler of the world. Jesus was. As near as we can tell, Mark was the first to proclaim Jesus as emperor over God's kingdom.

The Gospel and the Gospels

Young John Mark was the first to write an account of Jesus. He likely wrote his account (the book of Mark) under Peter's influence while they both were living in the capital city of Rome. The first words of Mark's book are these: "The beginning of the *gospel* of Jesus Christ, the Son of God" (1:1). These words set the tone for the rest of the book. *Messiah* was a Jewish political title. *Son of God* was a common Roman term. Both mean essentially the same thing.

Mark's Roman readers wouldn't have known much about Jewish messianic hopes or the history of ancient Israel. But the term *Son of God* would have been crystal clear. It was a title commonly used to refer to the emperor (like Americans know *commander in chief* means "president"). During the time Mark wrote his gospel, emperors were actually worshipped as gods. That's why Mark's introduction could have landed him in prison. He was asserting a new world ruler.

His gospel begins where Jesus's own life ended, by confronting one of the most challenging questions for an individual and a society: Who gets to be the boss?

The Gospel and the Church

The Gospels use some form of the word *gospel* twenty-three times. The rest of the New Testament has more than a hundred uses after Jesus's resurrection. Here's what that means. The gospel is not just the story of salvation Jesus brings *to* the church. It's also the message of salvation Jesus brings *through* the church. Simply put, the purpose of the church is to announce the message of Jesus to the world! Jesus is the emperor, king of kings, ruler of heaven and earth. The gospel is the good news that each of us can have our sins forgiven. Yet it's more than good news for individuals. It's the good news of a new nation.

We call this nation the kingdom of God because it's global and eternal. Jesus is our emperor and we're his representatives. This isn't merely our message; it's our responsibility. Paul put it this way: "If I preach the gospel, that gives me no ground for boasting. For necessity is laid upon me. Woe to me if I do not preach the gospel!" (1 Corinthians 9:16).

Because this message is of extreme importance, Satan works overtime to stop people from hearing it. From the time the Gospels were written until now, Satan and culture have joined forces against the message of Jesus's reign. This isn't just a fancy metaphor. Through his church, Jesus actually reigns in this world. It's our responsibility and privilege to be his messengers, announcing to the farthest corners of the globe a singular truth: we have a king named Jesus who sits on the throne in God's heaven to bring healing to God's earth.

Look around. Think about your friends and our culture. This world needs a good dose of *good* news. The gospel could bring healing to so many! Here's my challenge. Let the apostle Paul's declaration become your own: "I do not account my life of any value nor as precious to myself, if only I may finish my course and the ministry that I received from the Lord Jesus, to testify to the gospel of the grace of God" (Acts 20:24).

Key Points

- The word *gospel* literally means "good news." It was originally a political term.

- Mark was the first Christian writer to use the term. He did so in direct opposition to the emperor's claims to be the ruler of the world.

- Even more than the description of Jesus's life, the gospel is the announcement of the church. Our first priority is to proclaim Jesus as the one true king of the world.

This Week

❏ **Day 1:** Read the essay, imagining that you had never heard the gospel. How might you respond?

❏ **Day 2:** Memorize Mark 1:1.

❏ **Day 3:** Read John 2. Put yourself in the sandals of those who heard of Jesus for the first time. What was "the beginning of the gospel" like for you?

❏ **Day 4:** How is the gospel described elsewhere in the New Testament? Read Acts 20:24, Romans 1:16, and Galatians 1:6–9.

❏ **Day 5:** When it comes to Jesus and the gospel, would you say you are more ashamed or proud? What's one step you should take to be more public with your faith in Jesus? Take that step this week.

What Does It Mean to Believe?

The time is fulfilled, and the kingdom of God is at hand; repent and believe in the gospel.

—MARK 1:15

Do we even need to ask what it means to believe? Isn't it obvious? Actually, no. For many people, believing in Jesus simply means affirming what is true about him. It would be like agreeing that 2 + 2 = 4. But agreeing that Jesus died and rose from the dead doesn't always change a person's life. After all, even the demons believe that Jesus is God—and shudder (James 2:19). But they don't trust and follow Jesus. Faith goes beyond belief. It requires response.

So, what is biblical belief? Let's begin with the Bible's definition of *faith:* "Faith is the assurance of things hoped for, the conviction of things not seen" (Hebrews 11:1). This is important because just a few verses later we read, "Without faith it is impossible to please him, for whoever would draw near to God must believe that he exists and that he rewards those who seek him" (verse 6). Bottom line: read *faith* as "fidelity" or "allegiance" and you'll be on point.

Faith as Loyalty

In the Bible, belief is loyalty. Faithfulness. Fidelity. Commitment. Christ calls us to pledge our allegiance to him. Every soldier, teammate, and frat brother knows the weight of a pledge. This is the kind of loyalty that Jesus Christ demands from us. He's the Savior. But he is also the sovereign Lord. Which leads us to another aspect of our definition.

When we start talking about adding obedience to faith, many theologians (people who are really smart about God) get nervous. It feels as if we're claiming to be saved by what we do instead of faith alone.

That's a fair point. After all, the biggest difference between Christianity and all other religions is the fact that God saved us; we didn't have to work to save ourselves. When we understand this reality correctly, however, obedience is a natural outcome of our allegiance to Jesus.

Again, let's be clear. We're not saying that obedience saves us. We're simply saying that obedience is the natural and inevitable consequence of our belief. A pledge of allegiance entails a life of loyalty.

Nowhere is this more clearly stated than in the letter from Jesus's own brother James: "Faith by itself, if it does not have works, is dead. But someone will say, 'You have faith and I have works.' Show me your faith apart from your works, and I will show you my faith by my works" (James 2:17–18). He went on to give two examples of people who lived lives of loyalty. First, Abraham, the father of faith, *demonstrated by his obedience* that he truly believed God (verses 21–24). Second, Rahab, a prostitute, demonstrated her faith when *she shifted loyalty* from her comrades in Jericho to the invading Israelites (verses 25–26). (It's a pretty incredible story from Joshua 2.)

Paul said in Galatians 2:16,

> We know that a person is not justified by works of the law but through
> faith in Jesus Christ, so we also have believed in Christ Jesus, in order
> to be justified by faith in Christ and not by works of the law, because
> by works of the law no one will be justified.

Neither James nor Paul discredits works. Both insist that works be put in their right place. As an attempt to earn God's grace, works fail. You will never do enough good to earn your salvation. Yet when good works are "in Christ," they *demonstrate* faith in God's free gift of salvation. Paul said we were "created in Christ Jesus for good works" (Ephesians 2:10). Good works in Christ are inevitable expressions of our faith. Plus, when we obey God, our lives get better! In this sense, obedience is more God's kindness to us than our offering to him.

We clearly see this connection between faith and works every time the final judgment is described in the New Testament. Our works are what is judged since they're the expression of our faith. Jesus said it first: "Do not marvel at this, for an hour is coming when all who are in the tombs will hear his voice and come out, those who have done good to the resurrection of life, and those who have done evil to the resurrection of judgment" (John 5:28–29). Paul confirmed what Jesus said:

> He will render to each one according to his works: to those who by
> patience in well-doing seek for glory and honor and immortality, he
> will give eternal life; but for those who are self-seeking and do not obey
> the truth, but obey unrighteousness, there will be wrath and fury.
> (Romans 2:6–8)

Peter, another great apostle, agreed: "If you call on him as Father who judges impartially according to each one's deeds, conduct yourselves with fear throughout the time of your exile" (1 Peter 1:17). John said the same: "I saw the dead, great and small, standing before the throne, and books were opened. Then another book was opened, which is the book of life. And the dead were judged by what was written in the books, according to what they had done" (Revelation 20:12).

In conclusion, here's a simple test you can use to measure your faith. Those who are trying to earn salvation through works ask, "Is this all I have to do?" Those who are living out their allegiance to God ask a different question: "What else can I do?"

Simply put, faith works.

Key Points

- *Faith* should be read as "fidelity" or "allegiance."

- We're saved "by grace . . . through faith . . . for good works" (Ephesians 2:8, 10).

- Obedience (or good works) is not a means of earning salvation but an inevitable expression of allegiance by those who've been saved.

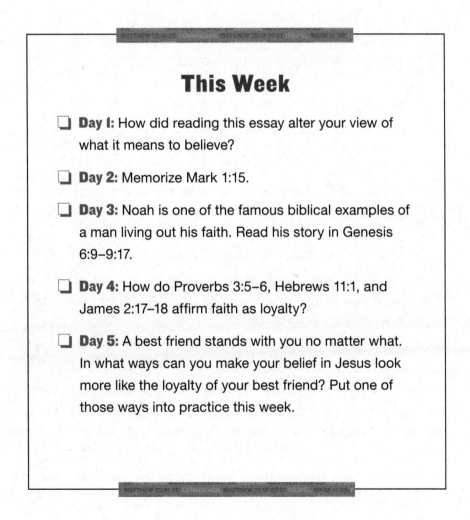

This Week

☐ **Day 1:** How did reading this essay alter your view of what it means to believe?

☐ **Day 2:** Memorize Mark 1:15.

☐ **Day 3:** Noah is one of the famous biblical examples of a man living out his faith. Read his story in Genesis 6:9–9:17.

☐ **Day 4:** How do Proverbs 3:5–6, Hebrews 11:1, and James 2:17–18 affirm faith as loyalty?

☐ **Day 5:** A best friend stands with you no matter what. In what ways can you make your belief in Jesus look more like the loyalty of your best friend? Put one of those ways into practice this week.

29

How Can I Find Rest?

The Sabbath was made for man, not man for the Sabbath. So the Son of Man is lord even of the Sabbath.

—MARK 2:27–28

Let's start with a little game. Set a two-minute timer, and then be perfectly still and quiet till it goes off. Seriously. We'll be here when you get back.

How was it? Did it seem longer or shorter than two minutes? Was it uncomfortable? Worrisome? Refreshing? However you feel about our game, you'll have to agree that our world doesn't slow down often. Just think about your average day. Alarms, texts, buzzes, beeps, tweets, likes, notifications, homework, chores, practice, dinner, work, . . . and, I guess, sleep (but probably with a phone nearby so you don't miss anything). We live with constant FOMO. We overcomplicate our lives because we fear missing out on an experience, the approval of friends, a scholarship, a relationship, something funny, the chance to graduate with honors—the list could go on.

But what if our overscheduled, hurried lives are actually the *cause* of our missing out?

Sabbath Is the Only Eden We Have Left

As a culture, we need help. We have no time for the things that matter most. Yet, from the very beginning, God knew our need to slow down—our need for rest. He gave us instructions to make sure we would enjoy it. It's called the Sabbath, and we need it now more than ever.

It's a rhythm that goes clear back to Eden:

On the seventh day God finished his work that he had done, and he rested on the seventh day from all his work that he had done. So God blessed the seventh day and made it holy, because on it God rested from all his work that he had done in creation. (Genesis 2:2–3)

God didn't rest because he was tired. He rested in celebration of His creation. Then he embedded the Sabbath principle in the earth itself.

The principle is simple: creation is most productive with a pattern of work *and* rest in proper proportion. For humans, that means we'll get more done in six days of work than seven. Our minds, emotions, and bodies need time to unwind, rest, clear the clutter, dream, and reenergize. If we don't rest, we actually get *less* accomplished because our creativity and energy are smothered.

When Adam and Eve sinned, human beings were kicked out of the Garden of Eden. We lost direct access to God. The earth itself was cursed and difficult to tend. Our bodies aged and died. The only part of Eden we still have full access to is the Sabbath. If we'll trust God and return to his plan for rest, our lives will be freer from the curse of Adam's sin.

Jesus Is Lord of the Sabbath

God's command to rest was simple: "Don't work on the Sabbath." The Jewish religious leaders took that command and turned it into legalism.[1] They made long lists of all the things people shouldn't do on the Sabbath. They were more concerned about the letter of the law than the intent of God's heart.

Jesus consistently rejected the traditional (man-made) Sabbath rules. On the Sabbath, he healed a man with a shriveled hand (Mark 3:1–6), a woman with a deformed spine (Luke 13:10–17), a man with swollen limbs (Luke 14:1–6), a lame man (John 5:1–9), and a man born blind (John 9:1–7, 14). Taken together, these healings make Jesus's point clear: humanity should be served by the Sabbath, not burdened by it. Or to use Jesus's memorable words, "The Sabbath was made for man, not man for the Sabbath. So the Son of Man is lord even of the Sabbath" (Mark 2:27–28). Jesus was reclaiming the Sabbath from religion and giving it back to humanity. But he was not simply blessing humanity. Jesus was putting himself at the center of reality so we could find rest in him! Listen to what he said: "The Son of Man is lord even of the Sabbath." To claim to control the Sabbath itself was to claim to stand equal with God. That's exactly the point! There is no real rest—no true peace—if Jesus is not Lord.

A Critical Warning About Sabbath Keeping

The Sabbath is not another rule to be added to your spiritual to-do list. More than a "have to," Sabbath is a "get to." It's God's gift.

Paul gave an important warning about rule keeping that we should apply here to the Sabbath (among other religious rules): "If with Christ you died to the elemental spirits of the world, why, as if you were still alive in the world, do you submit to regulations—'Do not handle, Do not taste, Do not touch'?" (Colossians 2:20–21). Paul's insight in that passage reveals the empty arrogance of legalism. What makes us right in God's eyes is the blood of Jesus. Religious activities are valuable only when they train us for serving others. And we do not earn gold stars by avoiding things. The old rules of religion are no longer needed since we're empowered by the Spirit of Christ.

The Sabbath is a pause in our week to remember these truths. It's a gift we receive, resting from work to refresh our souls, worship God with other believers, and reconnect with family and friends so we can invest in our communities. Believe it or not, when you add rest to the rhythm of your life, you will be *more productive,* not less. Your mind will be reenergized, your body revitalized, and your soul refreshed. This is the life God wants for you as much as you do.

Key Points

- Sabbath rest began in Eden as part of the order of creation.
- Jesus claimed authority over the Sabbath to restore its true purpose.
- Legalistic rules make rest a burden, not a blessing.

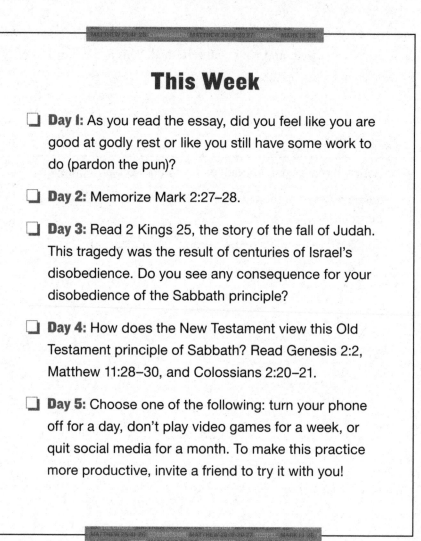

This Week

❑ **Day 1:** As you read the essay, did you feel like you are good at godly rest or like you still have some work to do (pardon the pun)?

❑ **Day 2:** Memorize Mark 2:27–28.

❑ **Day 3:** Read 2 Kings 25, the story of the fall of Judah. This tragedy was the result of centuries of Israel's disobedience. Do you see any consequence for your disobedience of the Sabbath principle?

❑ **Day 4:** How does the New Testament view this Old Testament principle of Sabbath? Read Genesis 2:2, Matthew 11:28–30, and Colossians 2:20–21.

❑ **Day 5:** Choose one of the following: turn your phone off for a day, don't play video games for a week, or quit social media for a month. To make this practice more productive, invite a friend to try it with you!

What Does It Take for Me to Be Great?

> Even the Son of Man came not to be served but to serve, and to give his life as a ransom for many.
>
> —MARK 10:45

What does it take *for me to be great?* For many years I would not even ask such a question. It felt sinful to want to be great. But Jesus never said it was. In fact, when his disciples asked him for positions of honor, he told them how to get those positions. So if you have ever wanted to be first chair in band, first string on the team, valedictorian, or most likely to succeed, you will want to lean into Jesus's answer to this question.

Good for you . . . Go for it!

The Request of James and John

As they were traveling to Jerusalem, James and John approached Jesus. They had their sights on the chief seats at Jesus's right and left. They had the audacity to ask Jesus to grant whatever they requested (Mark 10:35).

This infuriated the other apostles (verse 41)—not because it was inappropriate but because the others were envious. *All of them* wanted those seats! Jesus was also scandalized by their request but for a different reason. His reply is telling. The original Greek of "those who are considered rulers" (verse 42) could be translated like this: "those who give the impression of ruling." Jesus implied that those in power promoted themselves as rulers and sought popular support to substantiate their claim. These self-promoting leaders gave the impression that they were ruling, even though Jesus taught that God alone is the true ruler. Jesus was a different kind of ruler. Whenever he exercised his authority, it was for the benefit of the lowly, in teaching the crowds, healing people, or casting out demons (1:22, 27; 2:10–12; 3:15).

Jesus identified worldly leaders as "rulers of the Gentiles" (10:42). In Mark's book, two fit this profile—Herod (6:21–28) and Pilate (15:12–15). King Herod had John the Baptist beheaded to please his wife, even though he liked him. As for Pilate, he crucified Jesus even when he didn't actually want to. He caved to the crowds when they threatened him.

Neither Herod nor Pilate had control, even though they had power. They both caved to their subordinates because they feared losing that power. Here's the universal rule of rulers: those who present themselves as rulers are ruled by their desire to be seen as rulers.

What proved true in Mark's gospel is just as true today. Technology has changed, but political psychology hasn't budged an inch. Rulers are slaves to the power they hold.

Jesus is so different from politicians and other power-hungry leaders. He taught that "whoever would be great among you must be your servant, and whoever would be first among you must be slave of all" (10:43–44). We become great in Jesus's realm by serving, not attaining higher status and grabbing more power.

Jesus's Ultimate Advice on Leadership

"Even the Son of Man came not to be served but to serve, and to give his life as a ransom for many" (verse 45)—this is perhaps the most important thing Jesus ever said. It's certainly the most important leadership lesson he ever gave. Mark 10:45 is a summary of Jesus's biography. He's the Lord who died for the sins of the world. However, if we see Jesus only in this verse, we'll miss two critical leadership lessons.

First, sacrificial suffering is not merely what Jesus did for us but what he modeled for us. Thus, not only is the Cross of Jesus a gift to be received, but it's also a vocation to be accepted.

Second, Jesus saw his death as the means by which he would liberate Israel from the consequences of her sins in order to establish God's kingdom. Our role is to do the same thing in our own culture: bring the salvation of Jesus to people in our spheres of influence.

This whole theology of humility was nothing new for Jesus. Earlier he told an unlikely parable, recorded in Luke 12, about a master who went away to fetch his bride. When the master returned, his servants were to be ready and waiting. But the story didn't end the way anyone expected. Here are Jesus's own words: "Blessed are those servants whom the master finds awake when he comes. Truly, I say to you, he will dress himself for service and have them recline at table, and he will come and serve them" (verse 37).

Never had such a thing actually happened. No king, no governor, no other leader ever served his servants, especially not at his own wedding.

Until Jesus. The night before he died, Jesus actually washed his disciples' feet (John 13:1–17). Immediately afterward, he spoke these famous words: "If I then, your Lord and Teacher, have washed your feet, you also ought to wash one another's feet" (verse 14). If Jesus washed feet, no task is beneath any of us. Servant leadership began with Jesus. Any of us who want to be great had better get pretty good at rolling up our sleeves for the sake of those we serve.

Key Points

- Those who present themselves as rulers are ruled by their desire to be seen as rulers.

- The Cross isn't merely what Jesus did for us; it's an example of how we should live for others.

- Submission in service to others defines greatness for Christians. Jesus modeled this submission when he washed his disciples' feet.

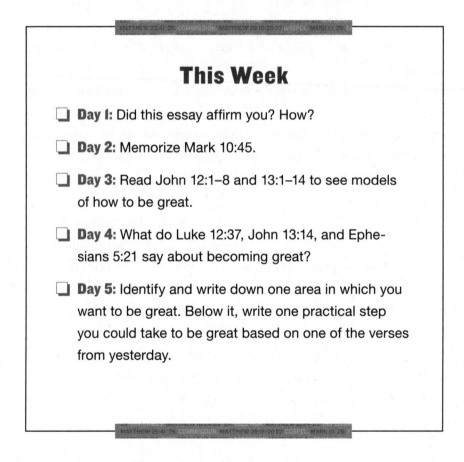

This Week

❑ **Day 1:** Did this essay affirm you? How?

❑ **Day 2:** Memorize Mark 10:45.

❑ **Day 3:** Read John 12:1–8 and 13:1–14 to see models of how to be great.

❑ **Day 4:** What do Luke 12:37, John 13:14, and Ephesians 5:21 say about becoming great?

❑ **Day 5:** Identify and write down one area in which you want to be great. Below it, write one practical step you could take to be great based on one of the verses from yesterday.

What Does God Care About Most?

Jesus answered, "The most important is, 'Hear, O Israel: The Lord our God, the Lord is one. And you shall love the Lord your God with all your heart and with all your soul and with all your mind and with all your strength.' The second is this: 'You shall love your neighbor as yourself.' There is no other commandment greater than these."

—Mark 12:29–31

What does the person you're trying to please the most care about the most? Perfectly sensible question, right? I mean, you don't want to spend all night memorizing a chapter in your science text if the teacher says he'll quiz you only on what you did in lab. The question matters in any important relationship, whether it's with a boyfriend or girlfriend or with your mother (especially when she's upset) or with God. So, *What does God care about most?*

Interestingly, this was the last question Jesus answered from his enemies before he died. We read, "One of the scribes came up and heard them disputing with one another, and seeing that [Jesus] answered them well, asked him, 'Which commandment is the most important of all?'" (Mark 12:28).

A year earlier, an expert in the Mosaic law had asked Jesus a similar question, one designed to trip him up: "Teacher, what shall I do to inherit eternal life?" (Luke 10:25). Jesus's response was brilliant. He let the lawyer answer his own question. Jesus answered with a question of his own: "What is written in the Law? How do you read it?" (verse 26). The lawyer answered, "You shall love the Lord your God with all your heart and with all your soul and with all your strength and with all your mind, and your neighbor as yourself" (verse 27).

Notice that the lawyer's answer in Luke 10 is identical to Jesus's own answer in Mark 12. Both answers reveal what is most important to God: love. Really, it's one command lived out in two ways:

God cares most that we love him and that we love our neighbors.

How Does One Love God?

Let's look at the original command in Deuteronomy 6:4–5: "Hear, O Israel: The LORD our God, the LORD is one. You shall love the LORD your God with all your heart and with all your soul and with all your might." In the original Mosaic command, we were to love God with all our being: heart, soul, and strength.

Sounds great! But let's dig a bit deeper. The heart is the center of feelings. It's more than emotion; it's the desires that drive our actions. The soul represents our energy. It's the life force that jolts us into action. Our strength represents our resources, not just our muscles. It's the total force of our money, time, influence, and relationships.

So, what does this mean? Well, several things. First, love is an action, not an emotion. I bet you know this deep down. A boyfriend or girlfriend who claims to love you but forgets your birthday and never wants to be around your friends is a fake. If we say we love God, we should show our love. How? By living lives that honor him and demonstrate respect for his commands.

The second conclusion builds on the first. We can't love God with only part of who we are and claim to have real love for him. If we go to church and are moved emotionally, we must also be moved by real needs around us. We can't read the Bible eagerly but not change our habits, hearts, and priorities. It makes zero sense to trust God with our eternity but not with our decisions today. And here's a big one: we can't trust God to forgive our sins while stubbornly holding on to grudges and bitterness, withholding forgiveness from those who've hurt us. (If you don't believe me, read Matthew 6:14–15.)

The third conclusion has to do with the command to love our neighbors as ourselves. By now, this truth should be apparent: the most obvious way of expressing our love for God is caring for our neighbors. Jesus couldn't have made this point more clearly than he did in Luke 10. The lawyer who asked him about the greatest command was trying to get off the hook for ignoring his neighbor. He was a lawyer, so he asked the *technical question* "Who is my neighbor?" (verse 29). He was actually super technical. The lawyer used the very specific definition of *neighbor*. He was trying to avoid loving certain people, wanting to love only those who might be more "deserving." Jesus answered with a memorable story. We call it the parable of the good Samaritan. (It's found in Luke 10:30–37 if you want to read Jesus's full answer to the lawyer's question.)

This lawyer was asking Jesus, "Who lives close enough to me that I have to care for them?" By the end of the story, Jesus had changed the question. It's no longer "Who is my neighbor?" but "Who is neighborly?" With that, Jesus also redefined *neighbor*. A neighbor is not someone who lives near us but rather anyone to whom we draw near. We tend to love those who are like us, whom we get along with naturally, or who just seem to get us. Those who are geographically, economically, culturally, or ethnically close.

Jesus's command is not that we like those who are like us but that we serve those who surround us. When we become the hands and feet of Jesus, it becomes clear whom we really love. By loving our neighbors—not just the people we like—we show that we love God with all we are.

That's what God cares about most.

Key Points

- The greatest command is to love God with all we are and with all we possess.

- Practically speaking, the only real way to love God is to care for our neighbors.

- A neighbor is anyone to whom we draw near.

This Week

☐ **Day 1:** Read the essay with this question in mind: "Does my lifestyle prioritize what God does?"

☐ **Day 2:** Memorize Mark 12:29–31.

☐ **Day 3:** Read the Ten Commandments (Exodus 20:1–17) and the parable of the good Samaritan (Luke 10:30–37). How do the expectations set out in these passages differ, and how do they overlap?

☐ **Day 4:** Think through Deuteronomy 6:4–5, Deuteronomy 10:12, and Luke 10:26–27. How do they differ, and how do they overlap?

☐ **Day 5:** What is one small habit you could practice that would make people a greater priority in your life?

Is God Jesus?

The Word became flesh and dwelt among us, and we have seen his glory, glory as of the only Son from the Father, full of grace and truth.

—John 1:14

I was never much of a baby guy . . . until I had kids of my own. Then I wanted to connect with them, so I got down on their level. I found myself playing on the floor with Legos, having tea parties with my daughter, and playing pretend with dragons and unicorns. I learned something about being a good dad: you get down on the level of your kids; you don't expect them to rise to your level. Because they can't.

I am so grateful God did the same thing for us. We call it the Incarnation. Every father instinctively understands what theologians have wrestled with. "Is Jesus really God?" they ask. Perhaps the better question is this: "Is God Jesus?"

I'm asking this question because of John 1:18, where we read, "No one has ever seen God; the only God, who is at the Father's side, he has made him known." What John wrote is right: our best chance of knowing God is through the life Jesus lived.

What I want to suggest is simple. If you believe that Jesus is God, then the God you believe in is different from any other religious deity. The Christian view of God is unique in three ways. These beliefs don't just tweak our view of God; they transform our lives and how we treat other people.

The Incarnate God Is Near

The first thing the Incarnation shows us is that God is near. He isn't messaging us from some distant galaxy. He revealed himself through the life and love of Jesus Christ.

True, some other religions teach that the divine is near. Animistic religions believe that the divine force is all around us: in rocks, rivers, animals, and trees. However, those religions don't promote a *personal relationship* with God. Their god is more like the Force in *Star Wars*—all around us but not close on a personal level. Several religions name God—Yahweh in Judaism or Allah in Islam. But for them, he's still not personal; he's distant.

Christianity is completely different. God is personal *and* close. We're taught that God came to us through Jesus so we could know God through our experience with Jesus. In fact, we're encouraged to pray directly to God using the most personal title, *Abba,* which means "Father" (Romans 8:15). Because of Jesus, God is near—personally available to every individual.

The Incarnate God Is Love

The Incarnation also shows us that God loves us. Other religions portray God as loving his people—though they're fewer than you think. In most religions, gods aren't much interested in humanity. But some gods do protect *their* people. For example, Yahweh rescued the Jews, and Allah rewards jihadists. Christianity teaches something entirely different: God loves us. God loves everyone. God even loves his enemies. "God shows his love for us in that while we were still sinners, Christ died for us" (Romans 5:8).

The first words of Jesus on the cross reflect this kind of love: "Father, forgive them, for they know not what they do" (Luke 23:34). That love gives Jesus the moral authority to command us to love our enemies (Matthew 5:44). He showed us how.

The Incarnate God Suffered

A third truth we learn from the Incarnation is that God can suffer. Compared with Greek mythology and dozens of other religions, this is an unusual idea. Their gods don't have to experience cold, hunger, loss, or heartbreak. They're above all that. But that's not the picture of God we see in the life of Jesus. He suffered just like the rest of us.

Actually, not much in the Old Testament predicted a God who would suffer, but two passages stand out: Isaiah 53 and Zechariah 12:10. Jewish rabbis found interpreting them extremely difficult. They didn't think God would become flesh, so they were confused about the concept of God suffering. However, because Christians believe that Jesus fulfilled these texts, we understand these ancient prophecies.

These three ideas about our God became evident when he took on human form in Jesus. More than being just interesting ideas in the history of religion, they are the most important truths we believe about God. Yet incarnation isn't only what happened in the life of Jesus; it's a model God intends for us to follow.

Why Does This Matter?

Do you want the best life possible? Live incarnationally as Jesus did. God is near; he has made himself available. Think what would be possible if you would just be present and available. Listen—really listen—to your friends. Take a break from technology and ask your parents about *their* day. Show up early for youth group, practice, or work and stay late. You would radically improve your relationships with those you care about the most.

God came near in Jesus to model how we can make ourselves present and available to others.

Second, God loved sacrificially—not just his friends but those who were opposed to him. "The Son of Man came not to be served but to serve, and to give his life as a ransom for many" (Matthew 20:28). Again, that's not merely what he did for us; it's a model he expects us to follow. In practical terms, that means listening more than talking, giving rather than taking, volunteering, bragging about others rather than self-promoting. In the end, sacrifice turns into gain.

Finally, God suffered. When we sympathize with friends who are suffering, we help them carry their pain. That is incarnation at work. Of course, we'd rather avoid suffering at all costs, and that's understandable. Pain is not fun. However, our greatest growth comes from our suffering, not from our success. We don't have to just *go through* struggles. With God, we can *grow through* them, allowing pain, loss, and inconvenience to build character.

John 1:14 is like a window; we see God most clearly in Jesus. But it's more than a window. It's a door. When we walk through it and live as Jesus did, we experience the incredible life God designed for our greatest good and the salvation of the world.

Key Points

- Those who know Jesus well will know God best.

- Nearness, love, and suffering are attributes of God seen best in the Incarnation.

- The Incarnation is not merely a theological truth; it's a practical model for successful relationships.

This Week

❑ **Day 1:** Think about your own parents as you read the essay. How have they modeled the Incarnation?

❑ **Day 2:** Memorize John 1:14.

❑ **Day 3:** Read Matthew 2 and Luke 2. What did Jesus have to give up and go through to come to us?

❑ **Day 4:** Meditate on John 1:18, 14:6, and Acts 4:12 to answer this question: Is God Jesus?

❑ **Day 5:** One day this week, go without your phone to be fully present with each person you are with.

33

What Is Real Love?

God so loved the world, that he gave his only Son, that whoever believes in him should not perish but have eternal life.

—JOHN 3:16

I have claimed to love many things: my wife; my kids; *Seinfeld;* my best friend, Larrie; a fire-grilled rib eye; Diamondbacks baseball; cold-brew coffee; my woodshop tools. Surely you know I love each of these in very different ways. That's why it is so confusing when we hear about God's love. What category does that fit into? It's an important clarification because if Christianity were reduced to a single word, it would be *love.*

In the English language we lump all kinds of emotions under the word *love.* The Greek word *agapē* is far more specific. *Agapē* means "unconditional and undeserved love." It's the love that causes people to sacrifice their lives for others. It's love offered freely, regardless of the recipient's merit or ability to repay.

Most people don't realize that this Greek word didn't get that definition until after John used it to describe God's sacrificial love in giving his son, Jesus Christ. The nature of love as undeserved, unchangeable, and sacrificial comes from the description of the gospel message of Jesus Christ. In this sense, Christianity created *agapē.*

One more thing. *Love* in our language commonly describes a feeling. In Christianity, however, love is first and foremost an action. Love is not how we feel. Love is what we do.

God Loves Us

The most famous verse in the Bible is John 3:16, this week's core verse. It's also the core of Christianity. But why does God love us? Contrary to what our mamas told us, it's not because we're so lovable.

God loves us because he cannot help it—he *is* love. "Anyone who does not love does not know God, because God is love" (1 John 4:8). Fish swim, birds fly, little girls giggle—they just can't help it. God loves for the same reason. It's not just what he does sometimes; it's who he is all the time.

This amazing truth caused the apostle Paul to write one of the most reassuring passages in all the Bible:

> I am sure that neither death nor life, nor angels nor rulers, nor things present nor things to come, nor powers, nor height nor depth, nor anything else in all creation, will be able to separate us from the love of God in Christ Jesus our Lord. (Romans 8:38–39)

According to John 3:16, God's love is so much more than raw emotion. It's an act of extraordinary self-sacrifice. God gave his own son for the sins of the world. Because God loved us so sacrificially, those who call themselves children of God are obligated to behave the same way toward all those around them (1 John 4:11).

The Bible calls that "lov[ing] your neighbor" (Matthew 19:19). The clearest explanation of John 3:16 is 1 John 3:16–17: "By this we know love, that he laid down his life for us, and we ought to lay down our lives for the brothers. But if anyone has the world's goods and sees his brother in need, yet closes his heart against him, how does God's love abide in him?" This agapē is not how you feel but how you help meet the physical and financial needs of fellow human beings, whether they are across the aisle on the bus, across the lunch table, or across the world.

In fact, it's impossible to say you love God if you don't sacrificially serve others. John's teaching originated with Jesus in the upper room the night before he sacrificed his life: "Greater love has no one than this, that someone lay down his life for his friends" (John 15:13).

We Love God

Jesus reduced the entire Old Testament law (which had 613 commands!) to two commands: love God and love people. Yet these are not separate commands. You cannot love God except by loving your neighbor. How could one treat God with sacrificial love? He doesn't need anything from us. You can hardly feed him, clothe him, or provide medical assistance. So, how can we express our love for God practically?

Every parent knows the answer: love his children. When we treat someone's children with kindness, it's the highest expression of love to the parent.

To love God's children, we are called to love three categories of people.

We love family. Family is a classroom of sorts where we learn how to behave in a way that matches what we say we believe. Paul commanded, "Husbands, love your wives, as Christ loved the church" (Ephesians 5:25). This love starts with parents but flows into every family relationship. Paul continued this command in 6:1–2: "Children, obey your parents in the Lord, for this is right. 'Honor your father and mother.'" John 3:16 is to be lived out first at home. We need to love and honor our families during car rides and conversations and in the way we do our chores. Loving God and our neighbors begins at home. Then it ripples out to our local communities and ultimately to the ends of the earth.

We love neighbors. Paul described the way we should treat teammates and classmates, friends and even strangers:

> Love is patient and kind; love does not envy or boast; it is not arrogant
> or rude. It does not insist on its own way; it is not irritable or resentful;
> it does not rejoice at wrongdoing, but rejoices with the truth. Love

bears all things, believes all things, hopes all things, endures all things. (1 Corinthians 13:4–7)

We love enemies. Probably the most shocking thing Jesus ever said was "Love your enemies" (Matthew 5:44). When Jesus said this, it was unthinkable. Two years later, he would exemplify that love on the cross. Remember the first thing Jesus said from the cross: "Father, forgive them, for they know not what they do" (Luke 23:34). One who forgives his enemies in the middle of a crucifixion has the moral authority to ask us to do the same.

Key Points

- Sacrificial agapē love is the core of Christianity and was actually "invented" by Jesus.

- Sacrificial love is what we do, not what we feel. And it originated with God.

- God's example of love in Jesus empowers us to love our families, neighbors, and enemies.

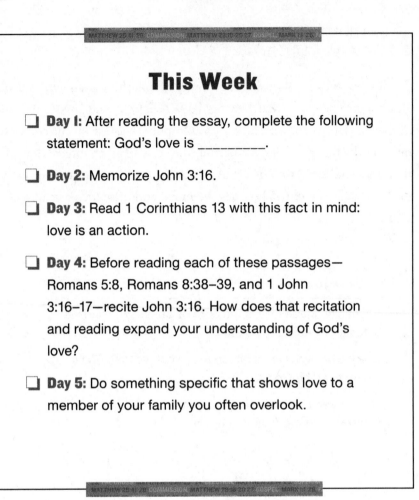

This Week

☐ **Day 1:** After reading the essay, complete the following statement: God's love is _____.

☐ **Day 2:** Memorize John 3:16.

☐ **Day 3:** Read 1 Corinthians 13 with this fact in mind: love is an action.

☐ **Day 4:** Before reading each of these passages— Romans 5:8, Romans 8:38–39, and 1 John 3:16–17—recite John 3:16. How does that recitation and reading expand your understanding of God's love?

☐ **Day 5:** Do something specific that shows love to a member of your family you often overlook.

What Does Real Worship Look Like?

God is spirit, and those who worship him must worship in spirit and truth.

—JOHN 4:24

Confession: sometimes I create awkward situations on purpose for my own entertainment. Twisted, I know, but you can learn a lot. Perhaps that's one reason I enjoy John 4 so much. It tells the story of two people—a man and a woman from very different backgrounds—who start talking. Without realizing what's happening, the woman stumbles from one awkward moment to another. By the end of the story, the whole amazing truth is standing right there for her—and us—to see.

The Father Is Seeking True Worshippers

I'm talking about the conversation Jesus got into with a woman at the local well. She was a Samaritan, from a people group despised by the Jews. She was alone, as was he. This fact made their conversation a bit awkward, especially when Jesus asked her to go get her husband. To Jesus's request, she simply replied, "I have no husband" (John 4:17). Jesus already knew that. He also knew that her current live-in boyfriend followed a string of divorces. Five of them. She was undoubtedly the subject of many rumors in that small town.

When Jesus revealed the details of her sketchy past, she was obviously eager to change the subject. So she asked him to settle a bitter debate between their peoples: Where was the right place to worship? Was it Jerusalem (the Jewish site) or Mount Gerizim (the Samaritan site)?

Her question launched one of the most important discussions ever about worship. Jesus's response is worth repeating:

> Woman, believe me, the hour is coming when neither on this mountain nor in Jerusalem will you worship the Father. You worship what you do not know; we worship what we know, for salvation is from the Jews. But the hour is coming, and is now here, when the true worshipers will worship the Father in spirit and truth, for the Father is seeking such people to worship him. God is spirit, and those who worship him must worship in spirit and truth. (verses 21–24)

What does real worship look like? She was focused on *where.* Jesus answered *how.* He repeated the answer so we wouldn't miss it.

Real worship is in spirit and truth.

Real worship arises from the Spirit and Truth (both words are capitalized on purpose). In the gospel of John, Spirit and Truth are more persons than virtues. Let me explain. Jesus is identified as the embodiment of Truth (1:14, 17; 5:33; 7:18; 8:32, 40, 45–46; 14:6; 18:37), and the Holy Spirit is described as the "Spirit of truth" (14:17; 15:26; 16:13). Christian worship honors the Father, as experienced through Jesus, by the indwelling of the Spirit.

True Worship Honors God in Our Hearts

The Greek word John used for "worship" here is *proskyneō* (John 4:24). It's actually a combination of two words that together mean "to kiss toward."

It's easy to imagine an adoring crowd throwing kisses toward a king passing through their village or a person kneeling before the king to kiss his ring. *Proskyneō* is used sixty times in the New Testament and at least twenty times implies bowing.

Here's why that's important. Many people equate true worship with the emotions of love or peace or joy. While those emotions can be byproducts of true worship, the New Testament equates worship with a different emotion: fear. This isn't the kind of emotion felt toward the subject of one's worst nightmare. It's the kind of fear felt toward a kind ruler or a good father. Maybe a better word is *reverence.*

Bottom line: true worship is recognizing God's position. He's our king, our sovereign, our Lord. He's not to be trifled with or taken for granted. So the posture in the Bible most commonly associated with worship is not hands lifted but heads bowed. In fact, the most common response to close contact with God is to fall flat, face toward the ground.

Fear is a better measure of worship than peace or joy is. Why? Because fear places God on his throne. From that position he can truly reign in our lives.

True Worship Praises God with Our Lips

The Bible talks about giving praise to God with our lips. Strictly speaking, we don't *give* God glory; we simply *recognize* his glory. This glory already belongs to God alone (Romans 1:21, 23). That's why it's so striking that throughout the Gospels, Jesus shares God's glory.

We verbally praise God in two ways. First, we recognize who God is—his character. Second, we recount what God has done—his actions. This kind of worship fills the entire book of Revelation (4:8–11; 5:9–14; 11:16–18; 19:1–8). What's more, it is directed to both God and Jesus as if they stand on equal divine footing.

True Worship Serves Other People

In the Old Testament, the priests worshipped through their duties (Hebrews 10:11). They offered sacrifices. They cleaned up blood. They lit fires and locked doors. Under the new covenant, all Christians serve in the new temple—the church. It's not about buildings but about people.

That's why we in the church feed, protect, counsel, and coach others. That's why connecting with the church is essential for personal worship. As Scripture commands, "Let us consider how to stir up one another to love and good works, not neglecting to meet together, as is the habit of some, but encouraging one another, and all the more as you see the Day drawing near" (verses 24–25). Worship by service triggers people to praise God when they see a Christian live well (1 Peter 2:12). Our actions cause others to compliment God.

Paul wrote, "I appeal to you therefore, brothers, by the mercies of God, to present your bodies as a living sacrifice, holy and acceptable to God, which is your spiritual worship" (Romans 12:1). Living this way is especially important because spiritual worship is the only thing we'll take to heaven (Revelation 7:15; 22:3). Worship is our eternal occupation.

What distinguishes Christian worship from other religious activities is the Spirit. The Spirit leads us to the Truth embodied in Jesus, who escorts us directly to the Father.

As the woman at the well discovered, that's what true worship looks like.

Key Points

- True worship recognizes God's position, which leads to our experience of appropriate fear.

- Praise is recognizing who God is and what he has done.

- Serving the body of Christ (the church) is the highest form of worship.

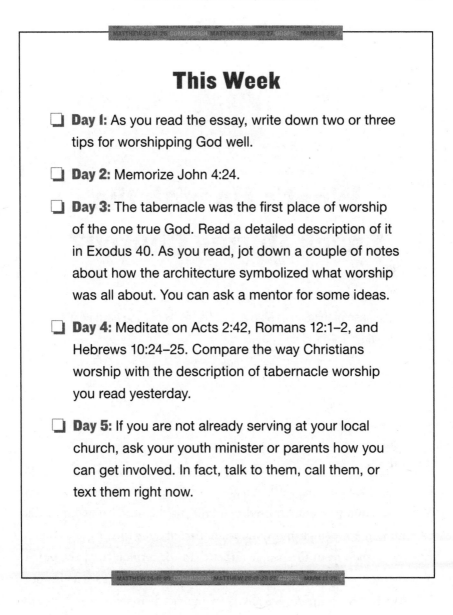

This Week

❏ **Day 1:** As you read the essay, write down two or three tips for worshipping God well.

❏ **Day 2:** Memorize John 4:24.

❏ **Day 3:** The tabernacle was the first place of worship of the one true God. Read a detailed description of it in Exodus 40. As you read, jot down a couple of notes about how the architecture symbolized what worship was all about. You can ask a mentor for some ideas.

❏ **Day 4:** Meditate on Acts 2:42, Romans 12:1–2, and Hebrews 10:24–25. Compare the way Christians worship with the description of tabernacle worship you read yesterday.

❏ **Day 5:** If you are not already serving at your local church, ask your youth minister or parents how you can get involved. In fact, talk to them, call them, or text them right now.

35

What's Up with the Snack During Church?

Jesus said to them, "Truly, truly, I say to you, unless you eat the flesh of the Son of Man and drink his blood, you have no life in you."

—John 6:53

I'm not proud of this, but when I was a kid, communion in church was a time for a mini nap. When it got quiet, I bowed my head and nodded off. As an adult, I'm embarrassed to admit that because I now know that communion is the single most important part of our gathering as a church. It is the sermon from the people rather than the sermon from the pulpit. Together we proclaim Jesus's sacrifice through the elements we consume.

This is why communion has been practiced in some way by every church in history. And this is why it deserves a conversation about what it means and how it should be celebrated.

Jesus established the Lord's Supper the night before he died (Luke 22:17–20). It was during a Jewish Passover meal with him surrounded by his closest friends. The church, since that time, has celebrated Jesus's sacrifice with a simple miniature Passover of bread and wine or juice. Paul's commentary about communion is still about the best explanation we have (1 Corinthians 11:23–26).

Communion Looks Backward

Communion has roots in the ancient Passover meal, going back to the founding of Israel. In fact, Jesus's word *remembrance* could be translated as "memorial."

With this observance, we don't just think about what Jesus did. Communion is more like a reenactment. Every year since the Exodus (fifteen centuries earlier), Jews had gathered in family groups around a table with a specific script and props. The unleavened bread represented the Israelites rushing out of Egypt. For Jesus, the wine represented the blood of the covenant. The Passover lamb retold the story of their escape from Egypt (Exodus 12). The table itself was the storyboard reminding Israel of their beginning as a nation.

Because Jesus fulfilled all Jewish history and hopes, he reinterpreted all the elements of the Passover in relation to himself, specifically his crucifixion that was about to happen. This new covenant, as he called it (1 Corinthians 11:25–26), would be formed around his body and blood. His interpretation must have come as a shock to his followers since nothing was more patriotic for Jews than Passover.

However, communion doesn't just look to the past; it also points to the future.

Communion Looks Forward

Paul said, "As often as you eat this bread and drink the cup, you proclaim the Lord's death until he comes" (1 Corinthians 11:26). This weekly memorial was a reminder in the early church that Jesus was, in fact, coming again! When he comes, there'll be an amazing banquet. "Blessed are those who are invited to the marriage supper of the Lamb" (Revelation 19:9).

We're not there yet. Nevertheless, Jesus predicted that it is coming, even as he celebrated the first communion with his disciples. In his own words, "I have earnestly desired to eat this Passover with you before I suffer. For I tell you I will not eat it until it is fulfilled in the kingdom of God" (Luke 22:15–16).

Because of the rich historical symbolism in this meal, we don't just reenact Passover; we proclaim the story of Jesus woven throughout Jewish history. In a real way, everyone who partakes of the Lord's Supper preaches the entire gospel message. It's an enacted sermon. Communion is a church-wide sermon without the preacher ever saying a word. Here's some great news about this sermon: we cannot proclaim it wrongly, since the elements themselves tell the story.

The Passover inaugurated Jewish history; the Eucharist will be its culmination at the marriage supper of the Lamb (Revelation 19:9) when Jesus will be our God with us (Immanuel) and we will be his people.

Communion Looks Inward

The Lord's Supper is the most inward element of our worship services. It's right and necessary that we reflect on our relationship with God. It's not that we wonder whether we're worthy to partake; Jesus's sacrifice alone is what makes us worthy. Rather, we prepare our minds and hearts for the sacredness of the celebration. It's no small thing to drink the blood of Jesus or eat his body through this symbolic meal.

It's a sacrament. Something spiritual, mystical, and powerful takes place when we practice it. Be forewarned: the cosmic Christ is present in the elements.

Communion Looks Outward

Communion isn't just about communing with Jesus. It's a communal meal we share with other Christians.

Originally communion was a full meal in someone's home where worship services were held (before separate buildings were built for churches to gather in). Consequently, the meal followed the preaching. The banquet hall was cleared and tables set up. The problem was that after the tables were set up, not nearly as many people fit in the hall, so most of the congregation ate in the courtyard. Who got to stay in the banquet hall? No surprise—it was the wealthy believers who'd earned their seats of honor before ever being baptized.

Old habits die hard. So, the poorer Christians went home hungry, and the wealthier Christians went home hammered (seriously): "In eating, each one goes ahead with his own meal. One goes hungry, another gets drunk" (1 Corinthians 11:21). This explains why the full meal was replaced by the "Chiclets and shot glasses" we have today. Paul explained, "When you come together to eat, wait for one another—if anyone is hungry, let him eat at home—so that when you come together it will not be for judgment" (verses 33–34).

Somehow we need to recover the "community" part of communion. Just as the original meal celebrated the birth of a nation, so this continued celebration is the mark of a Christian community. We are that community. And we have a responsibility—together—to take God's love to a broken world.

Key Points

- Communion is a Christian extension of the annual Jewish Passover meal.

- Communion is a reminder of Jesus's past sacrifice and future return.

- Though communion is a time for personal reflection, the name reminds us that it's a communal event binding the church body together in Christ.

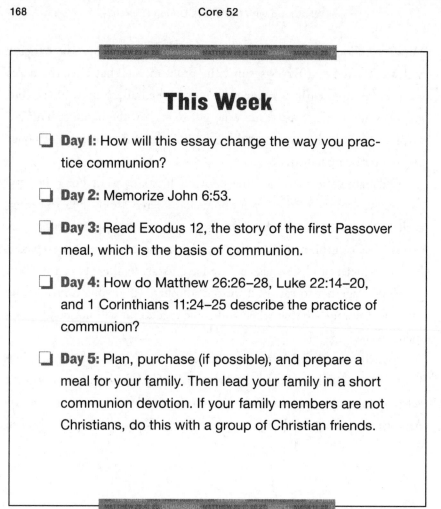

This Week

☐ **Day 1:** How will this essay change the way you practice communion?

☐ **Day 2:** Memorize John 6:53.

☐ **Day 3:** Read Exodus 12, the story of the first Passover meal, which is the basis of communion.

☐ **Day 4:** How do Matthew 26:26–28, Luke 22:14–20, and 1 Corinthians 11:24–25 describe the practice of communion?

☐ **Day 5:** Plan, purchase (if possible), and prepare a meal for your family. Then lead your family in a short communion devotion. If your family members are not Christians, do this with a group of Christian friends.

Can I Know I'm Saved?

I give them eternal life, and they will never perish, and no one
will snatch them out of my hand.

—JOHN 10:28

Can you feel it? In our culture most people want to blame somebody else for their problems and credit no one else for their success. It is my
observation that the healthiest and most successful people flip the script.
They credit others for their success and take ownership of their mistakes. I
see this pattern in Bible passages related to a famous debate over eternal
security.[1]

The Tension of Eternal Security

We're saved by the grace of Jesus Christ. End of story. It's not by our hard
work or knowing all the right answers. It's not because we did right and
avoided wrong. Jesus himself assures us that we will always belong to him:
"All that the Father gives me will come to me, and whoever comes to me I
will never cast out" (John 6:37). And again in 10:28, this chapter's core
verse, he spoke to the Pharisees, who were trying to intimidate his disciples
into abandoning him.

Don't miss this truth: Jesus fights for us!

Paul echoed Jesus's promise of security in the poetic crescendo of Romans 8:38–39, where he declared that nothing can separate us from the love of Christ. The guarantee of our security is none other than the Holy Spirit himself (2 Corinthians 5:5).

All this to say, our security in Jesus is certain.

There are, however, many passages that warn Christians not to let go of Jesus. The most obvious is Hebrews 6:4–6:

> It is impossible, in the case of those who have once been enlightened, who have tasted the heavenly gift, and have shared in the Holy Spirit, and have tasted the goodness of the word of God and the powers of the age to come, and then have fallen away, to restore them again to repentance, since they are crucifying once again the Son of God to their own harm and holding him up to contempt.

Jesus said, "If anyone does not abide in me he is thrown away like a branch and withers; and the branches are gathered, thrown into the fire, and burned" (John 15:6). Using a similar agricultural metaphor, Paul said, "[The Jewish branches] were broken off because of their unbelief, but you stand fast through faith. So do not become proud, but fear. For if God did not spare the natural branches, neither will he spare you" (Romans 11:20–21). More scriptures could be added, but these make the point.

So, there we have it: two groups of scriptures that appear to be in conflict. The first cluster assures us that we're secure in Jesus. The second suggests that we can abandon Jesus. How are we to manage that tension?

This isn't a Jesus-versus-Paul thing. Both Jesus and Paul emphasized our security in Christ *and* gave strong warnings not to abandon him. They are not contradicting themselves. Rather, they are making two separate but true statements.

Most preachers lean into one set of scriptures and explain away the other, often with creative mental gymnastics. Their arguments make sense for any single passage. But we've got to be careful about explaining away any part of the Bible. Instead, we should answer this question: "Can we hold in tension these two seemingly contrary positions?" I believe we can.

Somehow *Christians are eternally secure in Jesus while also having some responsibility for their own destinies.* To be clear, we'll never answer all the questions this statement might bring up. What we can (and must) do is understand and apply the practical principles behind these biblical truths.

Practical Principles for Understanding Eternal Security

Knowing what Jesus and Paul said is helpful for understanding; knowing why they said it is critical for life change. Here are some practical principles:

1. We should promote both sides to maximize ministry in real-life settings. The warnings against falling away are important for Christians who are lured away from Jesus by either suffering or success. Sometimes suffering tempts us to say, "Jesus doesn't help me," while success tempts us to say, "I don't need Jesus's help." The bottom line for those who suffer *or* succeed is this: hold on to Jesus because he is holding on to you!

2. Our perseverance in Jesus depends more on him than on us. Spiritual security isn't only or even primarily dependent on us. The Good Shepherd of our souls takes seriously his obligation to protect and keep his own flock. He's responsible for bringing us into the flock (John 6:44), and he's committed to sustaining us in it (10:27–30).

   Is walking away from the faith possible? Well, the Bible describes specific individuals who shipwrecked their faith and were handed over to Satan (1 Timothy 1:19–20). This walking away is called apostasy[2] (4:1). Nonetheless, it's next to impossible. Our good Father never lightly loosens his grip on his children.

3. Some pastors argue that a person can fall away. Others strongly disagree. Yet all of us know someone who used to claim to be a Christian but no longer does. The eternal-security side argues that this "ex-Christian" was never really saved in the first place, while the fall-away people say that this person apostatized. Neither side, however, doubts the state of people like Judas Iscariot (John 17:12), Simon Magus (Acts 8:18–23), and Hymenaeus and Alexander (1 Timothy 1:19–20). They agree they're lost.

   In light of what we know, *what should we do?* The answer is clear: help people find Jesus.

4. Both camps can be justly criticized for misguided messaging. Some people have heard a preacher say, "You are saved no matter what you do," and they misinterpret the message to mean they can sin without consequences. We have to admit that's the wrong message.

   On the other side, some preachers, overemphasizing our free will to abandon the faith, have caused people to live with fear and uncertainty. Clearly that's not a helpful or productive message either.

   If the Bible seems to promote both sides, it might be wise for Jesus's followers to do the same.

Key Points

- The Bible includes plenty of passages supporting both eternal security and apostasy.

- Christians need to hear both messages.

- Let's let the Bible speak on its own terms even if we can't reconcile apparent contradictions.

This Week

☐ **Day 1:** As you read the essay, underline three ideas you need to pay more attention to.

☐ **Day 2:** Memorize John 10:28.

☐ **Day 3:** Read the famous story of David and Goliath in 1 Samuel 17. How much of David's success do you think was based on God's protection, and how much was based on David's obedience?

☐ **Day 4:** Meditate on John 6:37, Romans 11:20–21, and Hebrews 6:4–6. Which of these passages speaks most to where you are right now spiritually?

☐ **Day 5:** Identify three people who helped point you toward Jesus. Thank God for using them to pursue you. Thank those people for pointing you to Jesus.

37

What Does the Holy Spirit Do for Me?

You will receive power when the Holy Spirit has come upon you, and you will be my witnesses in Jerusalem and in all Judea and Samaria, and to the end of the earth.

—ACTS 1:8

As a high school student, I knelt in a public park with a Pentecostal friend, pleading with God to give me the gift of tongues. He didn't. Nor should he have. Looking back, I realize that mostly I just wanted to feel special. I was asking for power for *me*, not to accomplish a work for God.

I learned a lesson from that experience. The Holy Spirit isn't interested in working *for* me. He wants to work *in* me and *through* me. Jesus himself said so:

> I will ask the Father, and he will give you another Helper, to be with you forever, even the Spirit of truth, whom the world cannot receive, because it neither sees him nor knows him. You know him, for he dwells with you and will be in you. (John 14:16–17)

Who is this Helper that Jesus promised? And how can we welcome him more fully into our lives? I invite you to kneel in your heart this week as we become students of the Holy Spirit.

Transformation: The Holy Spirit *in* Us

1. *Creation.* The Spirit of God played a central role in creation (Genesis 1:2). He was responsible for the very breath that gave life to humans, breathing into the nostrils of Adam (2:7). In fact, the Spirit of God is responsible for the breath of every living creature (Psalm 104:29–30).

   So, it just makes sense that once Jesus removed the curse of our sin, the Spirit could renew our access to the Father. Just as in Genesis 1:2, the Spirit still hovers over the chaos of our lives, seeking to bring about a new creation (or, perhaps more accurately, a renewed creation). It's what the Bible calls being "born of water and the Spirit" (John 3:5).

2. *Conversion.* The most important thing the Spirit does is invisible to the human eye. He seals us: "In him you also, when you heard the word of truth, the gospel of your salvation, and believed in him, were sealed with the promised Holy Spirit" (Ephesians 1:13). This idea comes from the ancient practice of sealing documents with a signet ring. Someone would press the ring into soft wax or clay, marking the item as the property of the king or dignitary. When we pledge our loyalty to Jesus by faith, there's a permanent change in our ownership.

3. *Sanctification.* Because we now belong to God, we're set apart for him and his plans for us. The Bible uses the fancy church word *sanctification* for this process (2 Thessalonians 2:13; see also Romans 15:16). We're declared forgiven the moment the Spirit seals us. But becoming like Jesus is a lifelong process. Sanctification is the constant work of God to line up our actions with Jesus's character and heart (1 Thessalonians 5:23).

Empowerment: The Holy Spirit *Through* Us

1. *Coaching.* The primary work of the Spirit in both the Old and New Testaments is communication. He's a talker! He has a million ways to speak into our lives but is probably clearest through the Scriptures. After all, he's the ultimate author (2 Peter 1:21). If the Spirit needs to, he can communicate directly with individuals in their hearts or minds (John 15:26; Acts 8:29; 10:19–20). He can also communicate through a third party, including but not limited to parents, preachers, teachers, counselors, coaches, friends, and even children.

2. *Skills.* The Spirit provides the tools we need to accomplish everything God calls us to do. Sometimes this power comes in the form of phenomenal miraculous interventions (Romans 15:19; Galatians 3:5). These could include healings (Acts 5:16), exorcisms (Matthew 12:28), and prophecy and speaking in tongues (Acts 2:4). These power tools are focused mostly on an individual who does something dynamic to expand the kingdom of God.

   The Spirit distributes his power throughout the church (Romans 12:6–8; 1 Corinthians 12:4, 7–12; Ephesians 4:11–13). Christians work together as a powerful force for good in this world (Ephesians 4:3–4). Because we need one another to accomplish the mission, we stick together.

3. *Character.* He also develops in us the *fruit of the Spirit:* "The fruit of the Spirit is love, joy, peace, patience, kindness, goodness, faithfulness, gentleness, self-control; against such things there is no law" (Galatians 5:22–23). Through these qualities, we carry out the commands of Christ to reach our neighbors with the message of salvation. The Spirit doesn't help us find the fruit; like a gardener, he cultivates it in our character. These qualities are a natural outflow of being truly connected to the Spirit!

4. *Support.* The Spirit has a sense for moving the right people into the right place at the right time. This happens more often than we

suspect, mainly in the process of evangelism, which involves talking to people about Jesus (Luke 2:27; Acts 8:29, 39; 10:19–20; 11:12; 16:6–7; 20:22). He guides us (Acts 13:2–4; 15:28), even giving us the right words to say (Luke 12:12).

Most of the time, the Spirit guides us by giving general wisdom about how to live (Ephesians 1:17). This is why the Spirit is called a counselor or coach (John 14:16–17, 26; 15:26). He provides encouragement to the church (Acts 9:31), strength to individuals (Ephesians 3:16), and help to the hurting (Philippians 1:19).

Sometimes (okay, lots of the time) life is tough. In those moments, the Spirit supports us, even when we're unaware of him doing so. He'll never leave us alone. In my experience, he's closest to us when we're closest to the heartbeat of the mission— announcing the good news of Jesus Christ.

Key Points

- The Spirit came to give us power. This power works *in* us and *through* us, not simply *for* us.

- The Spirit works in us through transformation: creation, conversion, and sanctification.

- The Spirit works through us in empowerment: coaching, skills, character, and support.

This Week

☐ **Day 1:** Read the essay. What is the most valuable thing, personally, that the Spirit does for you?

☐ **Day 2:** Memorize Acts 1:8.

☐ **Day 3:** Read about the Day of Pentecost in Acts 2, when the Holy Spirit came in power.

☐ **Day 4:** List what the Bible promises the Spirit has done or will do for you in John 16:13–14, Galatians 5:22–23, and Ephesians 1:13.

☐ **Day 5:** Read Luke 11:13 and do what it suggests.

38

Why Did Jesus Leave the Earth?

When he had said these things, as they were looking on, he was lifted up, and a cloud took him out of their sight.

—ACTS 1:9

Forty days had passed since the Resurrection. As Jesus stood with his disciples on top of the Mount of Olives overlooking Jerusalem, he gave them one final promise—that they would receive the Holy Spirit. Then he began to rise from the earth.

Weird, right? What if your teacher just started floating in the air on the last day of school?

This miracle marked Jesus's exit from earth. For his followers that day, this must have felt like abandonment. He was leaving? For good? Well, kind of. Yet he wasn't leaving them (or us) alone. His departure was actually exactly what they needed in order to fulfill their life purpose.

Jesus's Ascension Was Planned

Jesus had predicted his ascension: "No one has ascended into heaven except he who descended from heaven, the Son of Man" (John 3:13; see also 6:62; 20:17). He also said, "From now on the Son of Man shall be seated at the right hand of the power of God" (Luke 22:69). If Jesus was right when he predicted his death and resurrection, why should we doubt his prediction of his ascension?

Plus, Christ's ascension is affirmed throughout the rest of the New Testament. Paul said that God "raised [Christ] from the dead and seated him at his right hand in the heavenly places" (Ephesians 1:20). Paul also tells us to "seek the things that are above, where Christ is, seated at the right hand of God" (Colossians 3:1).

The author of Hebrews declared this about God's son: "After making purification for sins, he sat down at the right hand of the Majesty on high" (Hebrews 1:3). Peter wrote that Jesus "has gone into heaven and is at the right hand of God, with angels, authorities, and powers having been subjected to him" (1 Peter 3:22).

Other passages could be added, but these are enough to prove that Luke's account of the Ascension is not some weird isolated reference. It is a truth backed up by every New Testament author except James and Jude. These passages give us confidence: God planned the Ascension. But why?

Jesus's Ascension Is to Our Advantage

1. Jesus finished his work of redemption. Listen to his prayer to his Father: "I glorified you on earth, having accomplished the work that you gave me to do. And now, Father, glorify me in your own presence with the glory that I had with you before the world existed" (John 17:4–5). Jesus came to earth from heaven. He laid down his divine rights to live with us humans (Philippians 2:6–8). When he returned to heaven, it showed the depths to which he had descended as well as the heights to which he can raise us.

From that point of view, the Ascension is essential to putting Jesus in his proper place.

2. Jesus is preparing a place for us. On the night of his arrest, he promised his followers that he would go and prepare a place for them: "In my Father's house are many rooms. If it were not so, would I have told you that I go to prepare a place for you?" (John 14:2). On earth, Jesus died for our sins to make a way for us to get to God. Now he's preparing a place for us in eternity.

3. Jesus intercedes for us while seated at the right hand of his Father. He's not kicking his feet up, relaxing in heaven. Rather, he's seated as our advocate, pleading our case. We can imagine it as something like this: Whenever we sin, Jesus leans to his left, points to the scars on his hands, and says to his Father, "See these scars? These paid for that sin. Let's call it even." Paul painted the picture like this: "Who is to condemn? Christ Jesus is the one who died—more than that, who was raised—who is at the right hand of God, who indeed is interceding for us" (Romans 8:34).

4. Jesus sent us his Holy Spirit. Jesus's ascension opened the door for the Spirit's work of conviction, guidance, and support for the growing movement of God on earth. The Holy Spirit is no cheap substitute for Jesus. He is not the second string or B team of the Trinity. Rather, he has the same heartbeat as Jesus and the same mission as the Father. Yet he offers us one advantage that the resurrected Jesus couldn't: because of his nature, the Spirit can be equally present with every Christian at the same time. That's why Jesus said, "It is to your advantage that I go away, for if I do not go away, the Helper will not come to you. But if I go, I will send him to you" (John 16:7).

5. Jesus is preparing for his return. "Behold, he is coming with the clouds, and every eye will see him, even those who pierced him, and all tribes of the earth will wail on account of him" (Revelation 1:7). When Jesus returns, he'll bring to fulfillment God's ul-

timate plan. He'll bring human history to completion, usher in the Day of Judgment, and restore Eden in the new earth.

Key Points

- Jesus predicted his ascension, so we can trust that it was planned.
- Jesus is now in heaven, advocating for us before the Father.
- Because of the Ascension, the Holy Spirit was sent to continue Jesus's work.

This Week

☐ **Day 1:** Read the essay. Then in the margin, jot down two or three advantages you have because of Jesus's ascension that you hadn't really considered before.

☐ **Day 2:** Memorize Acts 1:9.

☐ **Day 3:** In Acts 1, read about what led up to the Ascension and what followed.

☐ **Day 4:** How do John 16:7, Ephesians 4:8–10, and Revelation 1:7 point to something bigger than the mere miracle of the Ascension?

☐ **Day 5:** Set a five-minute timer. Close your eyes and imagine Jesus enthroned at the right hand of the Father. If you're an artist, draw a picture of Jesus on the throne. Let that image give you confidence for today.

39

Why Should I Be Baptized?

Repent and be baptized every one of you in the name of Jesus Christ for the forgiveness of your sins, and you will receive the gift of the Holy Spirit.

—Acts 2:38

It was a pretty emotional day. I baptized my son when he confessed Jesus. It struck me in that moment that my job as a father was to point him to his heavenly Father (of whom I was a mere shadow). His baptism was a gift of God not only to my son but to our entire family. It connected him to the larger family of the church, who would now help me raise my son to follow Jesus Christ. Baptism turns out to be a big deal at a practical level. Since that day, I've seen this reality played out in thousands of families.

Is Baptism Essential?

Let's be clear: we're saved when the Holy Spirit marks us (see chapter 37 of this book). God determines when, where, and how we're saved. However, the Bible also teaches that baptism crowns the process of conversion.

Throughout the book of Acts, people publicly confessed faith through the act of immersion—being dunked all the way under the water (2:41; 8:12; 10:48; 16:33). That's why baptism is described as new birth (John 3:5; Titus 3:5), as clothing oneself with Christ (Galatians 3:27), and as a replacement for the Jewish entry rite of circumcision (Colossians 2:11–12). It's a picture of complete change. Complete submission.

Baptism in no way earns our salvation. Gaining heaven by getting wet? That's ridiculous! Baptism is, however, the appropriate expression of faith in God. We're aware that "faith apart from works is dead" (James 2:26). So the question is not "Should we respond to God's gracious gift of Christ?" but "How should we respond to God's gracious gift of Christ?"

When the Jews, convicted of their need for salvation, first asked the question "What shall we do?" the apostle Peter answered, "Repent and be baptized every one of you in the name of Jesus Christ for the forgiveness of your sins, and you will receive the gift of the Holy Spirit" (Acts 2:37–38).

Can Someone Be Saved Who Hasn't Been Baptized?

God can save people at any time and in any way he chooses. However, the New Testament assumes that believers will accept baptism as a gift from God.

If someone neglects this gift, it is much like a baby being born without passing through the mother's birth canal. The medical term is *cesarean section*. It is possible, but this isn't the first choice for either the woman or her physician. If, however, the life of the mother or child is at risk, it is the best choice. If humans are clever enough to figure out a C-section, don't you suppose that God, the giver of life, is too? God loves life, and he'll make a way! Even so, God's design (and command) is for every repentant believer to be baptized. It's a really great design.

What Are the Benefits of Baptism?

1. *Baptism makes us disciples.* The last command of Jesus was this:

   > Go therefore and make disciples of all nations, baptizing them in the name of the Father and of the Son and of the Holy Spirit, teaching them to observe all that I have commanded you. And behold, I am with you always, to the end of the age. (Matthew 28:19–20)

   Baptism is like acting out a prayer. Peter called it "an appeal to God for a good conscience" (1 Peter 3:21). Baptism is a way for us to perfectly demonstrate what God is doing in our hearts and minds. Our old life is buried. Our new life is raised with Jesus.

2. *Baptism connects us to God.* It's not merely a symbol. It's a sacrament. Symbols represent something; sacraments accomplish something. Sacraments connect us to heavenly realities.

   The water isn't magical, but the obedient act is mystical. Something actually changes in baptism. You can read the words of Paul for yourself. Through immersion we "put on Christ" (Galatians 3:27). Furthermore, we receive the permanent indwelling of the Holy Spirit: "He saved us, not because of works done by us in righteousness, but according to his own mercy, by the washing of regeneration and renewal of the Holy Spirit, whom he poured out on us richly through Jesus Christ our Savior" (Titus 3:5–6).

3. *Baptism saves us through faith.* For many, this is too strong a statement. After all, we're saved by grace through faith alone.

   I'm certainly not saying that we're saved by performing some good work of baptism. What I'm saying is that baptism is the appropriate biblical expression of authentic faith. Scripture supports this view: "Baptism, which corresponds to this, now saves you, not as a removal of dirt from the body but as an appeal to God for a good conscience, through the resurrection of Jesus Christ" (1 Peter 3:21). And Mark 16:16 says, "Whoever believes and is baptized will be saved, but whoever does not believe will be condemned."

Key Points

- Baptism is a gift from God and an enacted prayer.

- Baptism is the proper response to faith in Jesus, marking our new life in Christ by imitating his death, burial, and resurrection.

- Baptism connects us to God through faith in Jesus Christ and through the indwelling of the Holy Spirit.

This Week

- ☐ **Day 1:** Read the essay. If you have not been baptized, ask your pastor about this next step.

- ☐ **Day 2:** Memorize Acts 2:38.

- ☐ **Day 3:** Read in Exodus 14–15 how Israel passed through the Red Sea. Paul pointed to this event as a type of baptism (1 Corinthians 10:1–2).

- ☐ **Day 4:** Jot down the metaphors or images used to describe baptism in Romans 6:3–6, Titus 3:5–6, and 1 Peter 3:21.

- ☐ **Day 5:** Write down the name of a friend or family member who needs to "take the plunge," and commit to praying for that person.

What Is God's Solution to Racism?

He made from one man every nation of mankind to live on all the face of the earth, having determined allotted periods and the boundaries of their dwelling place.

—ACTS 17:26

We live in a nation that has historically suffered from deep racial tensions. Yet this isn't merely a national crisis; it's a Christian crisis. And since many churches are as deeply divided as their communities, racism is clearly a family problem. After all, our Father is being made to look bad because his children are practicing the worst kind of sibling rivalry.

God is the creator of *all* people: "He made from one man every nation of mankind" (Acts 17:26). The truth is even bigger than that. God has embedded his own image in every human soul (Genesis 1:27).

All of us have some sort of prejudice, and often it is hard to see in ourselves. Each of us is limited by our own experiences and by our human impulse to believe that we're right and "those people" are wrong. So, let's be careful when we talk about racism. But let's *do* talk. And listen. And act.

Racial Reconciliation in the New Testament

Eradicating racism is a big deal in the Bible because it matters deeply to God.

The book of Acts records the launch of the early Christian church. When we read Acts, we see that taking the gospel to every person is important to God. It's important because it's central to the Great Commission. When Jesus said to make disciples of all nations (Matthew 28:19), the Greek wording literally means "all ethnic groups."

Racial reconciliation through Jesus is a core principle in Paul's letters as well. Racism is a consequence of sin, so God is dead set on ending it through the sacrifice of Jesus Christ: "Now in Christ Jesus you who once were far off have been brought near by the blood of Christ. For he himself is our peace, who has made us both one and has broken down in his flesh the dividing wall of hostility" (Ephesians 2:13–14). This "dividing wall" was a literal barricade in the temple of Jerusalem barring Gentiles from entering. Archaeologists have found two segments of this wall with an inscription that reads, "No foreigner may enter within the balustrade around the sanctuary and the enclosure. Whoever is caught, on himself shall he put blame for the death which will ensue." Jesus came to destroy every barrier to any person coming to God.

God wants all people in his heaven, but not just to gather a great crowd. Nor does he expect us to evangelize other groups just because we're good people and need to be nice. It's not even simply that he values diversity or loves the whole world (which is, of course, true). The primary reason God wants all ethnic groups in heaven is that anything less is beneath his dignity. We evangelize the whole world because only then can our great God receive the praise he deserves from every people and tribe.

John put it this way in Revelation:

> Behold, a great multitude that no one could number, from every
> nation, from all tribes and peoples and languages, standing before the
> throne and before the Lamb, clothed in white robes, with palm

branches in their hands, and crying out with a loud voice, "Salvation belongs to our God who sits on the throne, and to the Lamb!" (7:9–10)

Racial Reconciliation in the Church Today

The path to ethnic unity is not necessarily through culturally combined worship services but through cooperative community service. Different churches must partner to take the tangible love of Jesus to their cities and neighborhoods. Suburban churches, with more resources, might work alongside inner-city churches whose experience and relationships could open doors to migrant workers, refugees, the generational poor, etc. This is only one example of literally thousands that could demonstrate races and ethnicities working together in view of the broader unchurched community.

In order for this cooperation to work, however, there needs to be a Barnabas (if you're unfamiliar with his story, it's recorded in Acts 11:19–30). This individual must be full of the Holy Spirit and respected in the communities that are serving together. And this person must be willing to risk his or her own reputation, as Barnabas did for the likes of Saul of Tarsus as well as for John Mark (9:26–27; 15:37–39).

Bottom line: racial reconciliation is hard work, but it's worth fighting for.

One thing is clear: racial reconciliation will not be brought about only through government programs, media messaging, sensitivity training, and integrated education. The way of Jesus is different. He calls for us to give up our interests to serve others. As long as we keep protecting our own interests, racial tensions will continue to fester.

There are two places where racism has mostly been conquered—the battlefield and the athletic field. Why? Because in sports or war, the enemy is clear. Our differences are unimportant because we have a unifying goal. The key therefore to racial reconciliation is to gather diverse groups under a banner that's bigger than themselves.

The good news for Christians is this: Jesus is our banner. Our cause is

Christ. If we'll focus on him, we will inevitably be brought together. This fact is precisely why only in the church of Jesus Christ will our world find racial reconciliation. There's just no other banner large enough to include our diversity.

So, we're morally obligated to use our influence, advantages, and resources to bring about racial reconciliation, especially in the body of Christ. We must humble ourselves to listen to and learn from people who are different from us. Giving priority to "the other" is an act of worship, reconciliation, and imitation of Jesus Christ.

Consider the challenge of James 4:17: "Whoever knows the right thing to do and fails to do it, for him it is sin."

Key Points

- Racism and prejudice are out of character for Christians.
- The gospel message and the Great Commission are designed to overcome sin of all sorts, including racism.
- The local church is the hope of the world, especially in overcoming racism.

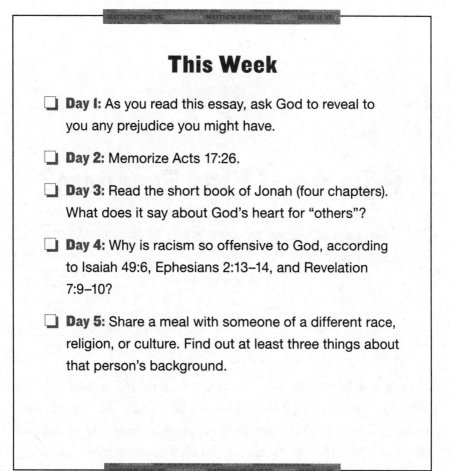

This Week

☐ **Day 1:** As you read this essay, ask God to reveal to you any prejudice you might have.

☐ **Day 2:** Memorize Acts 17:26.

☐ **Day 3:** Read the short book of Jonah (four chapters). What does it say about God's heart for "others"?

☐ **Day 4:** Why is racism so offensive to God, according to Isaiah 49:6, Ephesians 2:13–14, and Revelation 7:9–10?

☐ **Day 5:** Share a meal with someone of a different race, religion, or culture. Find out at least three things about that person's background.

How Can I Find Freedom?

There is therefore now no condemnation for those who are in Christ Jesus.

—ROMANS 8:1

In my early twenties I committed a sin that I held on to for another twenty years. It felt like a hidden ankle weight that kept me from living my best life—a shadow always in the background of my relationships, my prayer life, and my ministry. With that experience in mind, I can say with all my heart that I hope you aren't letting your past determine your future. You don't have to. God wants to set you free . . . *today!*

The Declaration of Freedom

Romans 8 is the single greatest chapter in the Bible for moving beyond the burden of judgment to the freedom of grace. It begins with a declaration of independence: "There is therefore now no condemnation for those who are in Christ Jesus" (verse 1). For you and me, that truth changes everything! Seriously.

Have we broken God's law? Well, yeah. Are there clear consequences for breaking it? Yep. But in Jesus, all that can be released. Paul explained why:

> The law of the Spirit of life has set you free in Christ Jesus from the law of sin and death. For God has done what the law, weakened by the flesh, could not do. By sending his own Son in the likeness of sinful flesh and for sin, he condemned sin in the flesh, in order that the righteous requirement of the law might be fulfilled in us, who walk not according to the flesh but according to the Spirit. (verses 2–4)

Notice that last phrase. It describes believers "who walk not according to the flesh but according to the Spirit." The Spirit in us takes over where Jesus left off. Christ fully and finally freed us from the law—not just its penalty but its pull. He showed us a better way, a higher path. As a result, the penalty of the law is destroyed and sin starts to look less attractive.

The only power that judgment has over us is what we give it. That's where the Spirit steps in: "Where the Spirit of the Lord is, there is freedom" (2 Corinthians 3:17). The Spirit is the missing piece of the puzzle. He's the key to living in the complete freedom we have in Christ.

The Spirit of Freedom

Being truly free starts with God forgiving our sin. Done! Or to quote Jesus, "It is finished" (John 19:30).

Our next step is to crucify our old selves. This is the slow and sometimes strenuous task of living by the Spirit rather than by the instincts of our old nature. Paul addressed this process, too, in Romans 8:

> If the Spirit of him who raised Jesus from the dead dwells in you, he who raised Christ Jesus from the dead will also give life to your mortal bodies through his Spirit who dwells in you.
>
> So then, brothers, we are debtors, not to the flesh, to live according to the flesh. For if you live according to the flesh you will die, but if by

the Spirit you put to death the deeds of the body, you will live. (verses 11–13)

Pretty simple, right? But just because something is simple doesn't make it easy. Roadblocks keep us from living this out.

The main roadblock is actually our own thoughts—for example, when we believe that our deeds and desires determine our identity. We think that since we sinned, we must be sinners. But that assumption is one of the most destructive lies of the Evil One. Our true identity is in our created nature, not our fallen nature. We were created by God; therefore, we're his children. We were redeemed (bought back) by Jesus; therefore, we're his possession. We were filled with the Holy Spirit; therefore, we're saints.

If we can just believe what God says about us, we can better follow his commands. *This is exactly why one of the main jobs of the Spirit within us is to convince us we're not who we naturally think we are:* "You did not receive the spirit of slavery to fall back into fear, but you have received the Spirit of adoption as sons, by whom we cry, 'Abba! Father!'" (verse 15). When we hear the Spirit's whisper, we can shout, "Abba! Father!"

If God has forgiven you in Jesus, stop believing the lies Satan is feeding you. You are a child of God.

Furthermore, "The Spirit helps us in our weakness. For we do not know what to pray for as we ought, but the Spirit himself intercedes for us with groanings too deep for words" (verse 26). When we lie breathless on our backs, unable to pray, the Holy Spirit intervenes with a wordless prayer. His groaning on our behalf says all that needs to be expressed to move God to action.

The Fight for Freedom

God paid the ultimate price for us. His love knows no bounds. We can therefore rest assured that he'll never cease loving us, he'll never release us, nor will he allow anything to separate us from him.

Romans 8 closes with one of the most powerful messages in all the Bible:

> If God is for us, who can be against us? . . . Who shall bring any charge against God's elect? It is God who justifies. Who is to condemn? Christ Jesus is the one who died—more than that, who was raised—who is at the right hand of God, who indeed is interceding for us. Who shall separate us from the love of Christ? Shall tribulation, or distress, or persecution, or famine, or nakedness, or danger, or sword? . . .
>
> No, in all these things we are more than conquerors through him who loved us. For I am sure that neither death nor life, nor angels nor rulers, nor things present nor things to come, nor powers, nor height nor depth, nor anything else in all creation, will be able to separate us from the love of God in Christ Jesus our Lord. (verses 31, 33–35, 37–39)

Key Points

- Our pasts don't have to determine our futures.
- God, through Jesus, has provided everything necessary for our freedom.
- In the Spirit we can experience full freedom.

This Week

☐ **Day 1:** While reading the essay, circle the Bible verses that strike you the most.

☐ **Day 2:** Memorize Romans 8:1.

☐ **Day 3:** Read John 8:1–11. How does this woman's story of freedom mirror your own?

☐ **Day 4:** Meditate on Romans 8:15, 28, 37. Which of these verses is most important for you to receive?

☐ **Day 5:** Write on a piece of paper every sin you keep holding against yourself. Then burn the paper as a symbol of releasing your past to God's grace. Seriously. Be careful, but have fun!

How Can I Change?

Do not be conformed to this world, but be transformed by the renewal of your mind, that by testing you may discern what is the will of God, what is good and acceptable and perfect.

—ROMANS 12:2

If you're like me, you've got some things in your life you're not proud of. Some skeletons in the closet. Regrets and mistakes. (I shared some of my story in the previous essay.) But there is good news! Your struggles today or in the past don't have to determine your future. You can change. We all can change.

Change isn't easy. But it's not complicated. The Bible shows us three simple steps to change: (1) believe God's promise of change, (2) receive his power to change, and (3) accept the challenge to change.

Believe God's Promise of Change

Jesus's sacrifice frees us so his Spirit can send us. No matter your darkness, God can bring light. If you believe his promise, confess your need.

This process is easier than you might think: "If you confess with your mouth that Jesus is Lord and believe in your heart that God raised him from the dead, you will be saved. For with the heart one believes and is justified, and with the mouth one confesses and is saved" (Romans 10:9–10). Your past is no longer a barrier to your best future: "If anyone is in Christ, he is a new creation. The old has passed away; behold, the new has come" (2 Corinthians 5:17).

Receive His Power to Change

When you're stuck in old ways, change can seem impossible. The urges inside you just feel too strong. To make things worse, you're up against the lies of our culture. Plus, our invisible enemy, Satan, is powerful and seductive. He and his demons have been crafting their strategy for thousands of years. How can we possibly get past these obstacles? We must receive God's power.

1. *God's love overcomes our internal impulses.* Anyone who has ever fallen in love knows this to be true. A guy who didn't know what deodorant was all of a sudden drops fifty dollars on cologne. A girl who never liked sports falls in love and suddenly finds herself watching the game every week. In the same way, when we experience the transformational power of God's acceptance, it changes our interests.

2. *Our Christian community overcomes our culture.* God created us for conformity. Now, that's a terrible thing if you follow fools into self-destructive behavior. Just picture some of the stuff that happens at your school in the name of fitting in. But when we choose to fit in with or conform to the right crowd, it leads to powerful and transformative community. The right mentors, coaches, and friends bring out the best in us. When we join the right community, we accomplish more together *and* live healthier lives.

   This is why regular church attendance is so important. It reinforces the values that fortify our lives. It's not just—or even primarily—about the lessons we learn but about the connections we make. We're better together.

3. *God's Spirit in us overcomes the demons against us.* "Little children, you are from God and have overcome them, for he who is in you is greater than he who is in the world" (1 John 4:4). Satan is certainly powerful, but Jesus is far more powerful! And you have the Spirit of God inside you as an advocate. You have more power available through Jesus than Satan can ever hope to use against you! This truth should build confidence and grow grit in your soul.

Accept the Challenge to Change

We all have areas of our lives not yet submitted to Jesus Christ. It might be an addiction to a substance or a screen. It could be an uncontrolled tongue, whether speaking, texting, or posting. Perhaps it's self-harm or doubt. Before moving on, identify one practice (not three or five) that you'll commit to changing. Pause and do this now before moving to the next paragraph.

Whatever you just identified will be difficult to change. Don't be naive and assume that because you're a Christian, you can just knock it out. Transformational change is tough, but as believers we have all the resources needed.

Take another look at our core verse:

Do not be conformed to this world, but be transformed by the renewal of your mind, that by testing you may discern what is the will of God, what is good and acceptable and perfect. (Romans 12:2)

Let's geek out for a bit. The Greek for "conformed" is *syschēmatizō.* Right in the middle you'll see the source of our English word *schematic,* as in diagrams or designs. Our culture has schematics: materialism, entertainment, individualism, and sensuality. These values are "in the air," so to speak. We naturally drift toward them unless we intentionally resist their effects. How can we do so?

God gives us four sources of strength for our journey of transformation:

1. *Scripture.* Studies like this book help us think differently about life. If the Word of God isn't in you, the world around you will consume you.

2. *Music.* Worship music exalts God, and we get caught in the updraft. The heavier your baggage, the more worship you'll need. Trust me, it's not "just a song." Music takes us places, so be careful where your music is taking you.

3. *Service.* Jesus still shows up among the excluded—the orphan, the trafficked, the poor. When we serve where he is, we experience his presence.

4. *Fellowship.* As we gather to worship, pray, and proclaim God's Word, the whole is greater than the sum of its parts. We're transformed simply by putting ourselves in God's community.

There's no shortcut to radical transformation. The cost is always high and the process often painful. But the benefits of genuine change are more gratifying than the sacrifice is difficult.

Key Points

- Radical transformation is possible. The Bible promises this!
- The power to change is found in God's love, his people, and his Spirit.
- God gives us strength for the journey of transformation through Scripture, music, service, and fellowship.

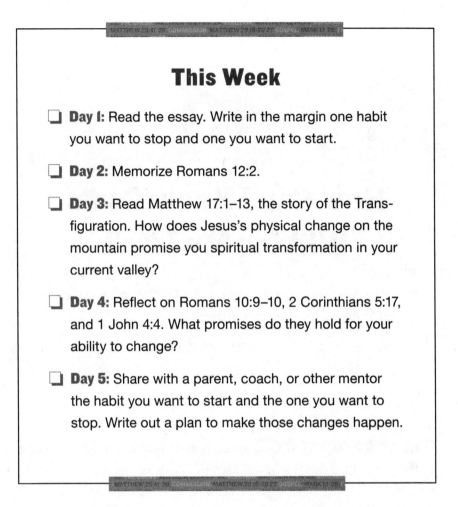

This Week

❏ **Day 1:** Read the essay. Write in the margin one habit you want to stop and one you want to start.

❏ **Day 2:** Memorize Romans 12:2.

❏ **Day 3:** Read Matthew 17:1–13, the story of the Trans-figuration. How does Jesus's physical change on the mountain promise you spiritual transformation in your current valley?

❏ **Day 4:** Reflect on Romans 10:9–10, 2 Corinthians 5:17, and 1 John 4:4. What promises do they hold for your ability to change?

❏ **Day 5:** Share with a parent, coach, or other mentor the habit you want to start and the one you want to stop. Write out a plan to make those changes happen.

How Can I Know God's Will for My Life?

"Who has understood the mind of the Lord so as to instruct him?" But we have the mind of Christ.

—1 CORINTHIANS 2:16

Can we know what God wants us to do with our lives? The simple answer is yes. God wants to reveal his will to us more than we want to receive it. In fact, the Bible is packed full of verses that both reveal God's general will for us and guide our most important decisions.

Let's start with the big picture (what we're calling God's general will).

God's Will for Us (and Everyone)

First, he wants us to be saved. God "is patient toward you, not wishing that any should perish, but that all should reach repentance" (2 Peter 3:9). But being saved means way more than going to heaven when we die. Our holiness actually leads to better, healthier lives: "This is the will of God, your sanctification: that you abstain from sexual immorality" (1 Thessalonians 4:3). Sexual purity is just one example; God longs for our good in every area. He always has a good reason behind the rules! Paul said, "Rejoice always, pray without ceasing, give thanks in all circumstances; for this is the will of God in Christ Jesus for you" (5:16–18).

Second, God desires us to do good so our lives will be an authentic witness to others: "This is the will of God, that by doing good you should put to silence the ignorance of foolish people" (1 Peter 2:15).

Conclusion: clearly God's general will is for us to be saved and witness to others.

God's Will Just for You

But what about daily decisions like how to counsel a friend, how to spend your time, whom to date, and how to drive? What about major life decisions like what college to attend and what career to pursue? Can we know what God wants us to do in specific situations that the Bible doesn't address? The short answer is yes!

Imagine, for a moment, you could know what God is thinking. Wouldn't you love to have access to his perspective to help you make decisions? Surprise! Paul said we can. We can actually know the deep and hidden thoughts of God. This is beyond extraordinary. How is that even possible? How could we ever get on the same wavelength as the Creator of the universe?

Paul wrote, "Who knows a person's thoughts except the spirit of that person, which is in him? So also no one comprehends the thoughts of God except the Spirit of God" (1 Corinthians 2:11). We've all struggled to know what someone else is thinking. First dates are awkward. Job interviews are intimidating. Your date across the table or interviewer across the desk gives you a courteous smile. But deep down, you don't know whether the person is impressed or thinks you're an idiot. That's why even best friends sometimes have conflict. We think we know what another person is thinking, but all too often we're wrong. In reality, we can't know with certainty what anyone else is thinking.

Yet listen to what Paul said next:

We have received not the spirit of the world, but the Spirit who is from
God, that we might understand the things freely given us by God.
And we impart this in words not taught by human wisdom but taught
by the Spirit, interpreting spiritual truths to those who are spiritual.
(verses 12–13)

What in the world do these verses mean?

Two things stand out. First, this access isn't open equally to every
Christian. Some are saved but don't have the ability to think spiritually.
Why? Because they're still practicing lifestyles that don't match God's priorities. Jesus said it this way: "If anyone's will is to do God's will, he will
know whether the teaching is from God or whether I am speaking on my
own authority" (John 7:17). Translated, that means *if we do God's will that
we do know, then we can discover his will for what we don't yet know.* Read
that statement again. It's an important truth. The more we understand the
Bible, the less entangled we will be in habitual sin.

Second, a more common problem is that we just don't know what the
Scriptures teach. Far too many Christians have no idea what the Bible actually says. But we can fix that problem. That's what this book is all about!
Knowing the basics of God's Word allows us to ask honestly whether our
lives are in line with God's priorities. If we allow the Bible to instruct us
and change our habits, we have the real possibility of having the mind of
Christ.

In 1 Corinthians 2:16 we come to one of the most stunning statements
of the Bible (Paul was paraphrasing Isaiah 40:13): "Who has understood
the mind of the Lord so as to instruct him?" The answer is obvious: no one!
No one can instruct God as if he needed our opinion. We'll never make
some observation that causes him to throw his head back and say, "I never
knew that!"

Yet the verse isn't finished. In a breathtaking conclusion, Paul said,
"But we have the mind of Christ."

Let me say this as simply as I can: if you're a Spirit-filled follower of
Jesus Christ and you align your life with his priorities, the more Scripture

you consume, the more potential you have to access the thoughts of God. The more you obey God's Word, the more you'll recognize his voice and understand his will for every decision you face.

Key Points

- God's general will for us is crystal clear, especially when it comes to morality.

- The Holy Spirit reveals God's will about our personal choices as we obey his Word.

- Disobedience blinds us to God's will, while obedience makes us more aware of what he wants for us.

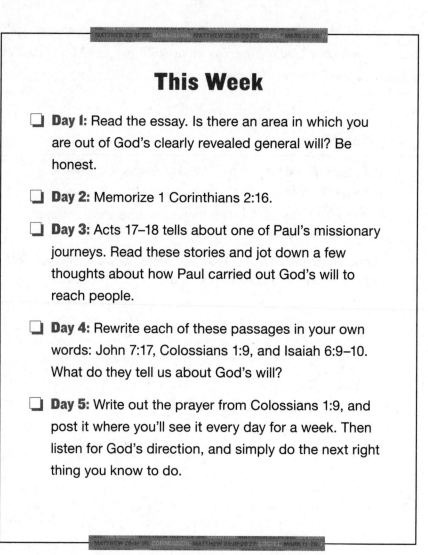

This Week

☐ **Day 1:** Read the essay. Is there an area in which you are out of God's clearly revealed general will? Be honest.

☐ **Day 2:** Memorize 1 Corinthians 2:16.

☐ **Day 3:** Acts 17–18 tells about one of Paul's missionary journeys. Read these stories and jot down a few thoughts about how Paul carried out God's will to reach people.

☐ **Day 4:** Rewrite each of these passages in your own words: John 7:17, Colossians 1:9, and Isaiah 6:9–10. What do they tell us about God's will?

☐ **Day 5:** Write out the prayer from Colossians 1:9, and post it where you'll see it every day for a week. Then listen for God's direction, and simply do the next right thing you know to do.

Did Jesus Really Rise from the Dead?

If Christ has not been raised, then our preaching is in vain and your faith is in vain.

—1 CORINTHIANS 15:14

Can I be honest? Some days I doubt almost everything about my faith. And truthfully, some days I even *want* to doubt. There is one thing, however, that I've never doubted (and, believe me, I've tried to explain it away). It is the bodily resurrection of Jesus Christ. This is the foundation of Christianity and why, even on my worst days, I've never abandoned the faith. I want to share with you the four facts about the Resurrection that confirm my faith. In fact, virtually every historian who has studied the first-century world agrees with all four.

1. *Jesus was executed by crucifixion.* This fact is recorded by seven New Testament authors—Matthew, Mark, Luke, John, Paul, Peter, and the author of Hebrews—as well as two nonbiblical historians, Josephus and Tacitus.

Plus, all four gospels state that Joseph of Arimathea—a member of the Sanhedrin, the ruling council of Jews in Jerusalem—provided a tomb for Jesus's burial. There is absolutely no way they would have claimed that a Sanhedrin member had sympathized with Jesus if it weren't true. To invent that kind of a lie would have been extremely dangerous.

2. *The tomb was empty.* The whole Bible agrees on this fact. Anyone who denies it has to explain why Jesus's tomb was never honored by his followers. Considering the Jewish practice of honoring graves, this exception is inconceivable without an empty tomb.

Additionally, the central teaching of the early church was the bodily resurrection of Jesus (Acts 17:32; 1 Corinthians 15:3–4). It's unthinkable that the Christian church, which began in the very city of Jesus's execution, could have made any headway had his tomb still been occupied. Surely someone would have produced the body and squashed the emerging movement.

Some suggest that the apostles' experience was a hallucination or a vision. But there's virtually no example of Jews—or anyone else for that matter—talking about a spiritual or mystical resurrection. Resurrection always meant that a dead body came back to life. Sure, people had visions and dreams, but they called them what they were: angelic visitations (Acts 12:14–15). They never referred to them as resurrections.

Finally, some people claim that Jesus's body was stolen. Matthew recorded the story of the guards reporting that the disciples took the body (28:11–15). The question here is "Who started the rumor, and why?" Christians never would have invented a story in which they stole the body. Plus, moving the body would have dishonored Jesus's burial. Jesus's followers never would have done that. And Roman soldiers could have been killed for losing their "prisoner," so it's ridiculous to think they would have made up the story. The only explanation for who started the rumor is that it was the chief priests and elders (verses 11–13), just as Matthew said. This makes sense. If the tomb weren't empty, they would have had no need to accuse the disciples of stealing the body.

All indications are that the tomb was, in fact, empty.

3. *The apostles believed that Jesus had appeared to them in a tangible body.* Neither Greeks nor Romans even desired resurrection. They considered the body a prison of the soul. We can be confident, then, that Christians didn't invent this story to impress their neighbors.

Many Jews, on the other hand, did believe in physical resurrection. Except they believed it would be corporate and at the end of time, not right in the middle of history. Jesus's resurrection was radically different from the dominant belief in Judaism. So, once again, why would Christians invent this story to impress their neighbors?

And then there are the disciples. Whatever experience they had—or thought they had—led them to conclude Jesus was resurrected (Matthew 28:9; Luke 24:36–43). And that conclusion radically transformed them! Peter went from being a coward (Matthew 26:69–75) to being a bold preacher (Acts 2:14–40). James, the half brother of Jesus, went from being a critic (John 7:1–9) to being the key leader of the Jerusalem church (Acts 15:13; 21:18; Galatians 2:9). Thomas went from being a skeptic to being a worshipper (John 20:24–28) with his profound declaration of Jesus's deity: "My Lord and my God!" (verse 28). Then there's Paul, who went from being the church's chief persecutor to being its most effective promoter (Galatians 1:11–16; 1 Corinthians 9:1; 15:8–10).

In short, something extraordinary happened to these men to cause their lives to be so radically transformed.

4. *The Christian church was founded.* If that statement sounds obvious to you, consider this fact: every Jewish movement in the first century died when its founder died, unless the nearest family member carried it on. With Jesus, though, it's different. He was a

messianic leader who was arrested and crucified—the most shameful punishment available. This execution should have crushed the movement (Luke 24:21). Yet fifty days later, the church exploded in the very city where Jesus had been executed. Even more, the shameful cross became the centerpiece of the entire movement. Then there's communion, the ritual eating of Jesus's flesh and drinking of his blood. Who would memorialize a dead Messiah with such cannibalistic symbolism?

Likewise, the practice of baptism must be explained. The form of baptism itself assumes belief in resurrection since it is a symbolic burial and resurrection (Romans 6:4–5). This Christian entry rite replaced Jewish circumcision (Colossians 2:11–12). Circumcision was one of the cherished marks of Judaism. Replacing it with baptism for Gentile Christians was an enormous shift! It would be like someone in your church replacing the image of Jesus on the cross with a statue of Buddha. Can you imagine the controversy that would incite?

Finally, what would cause a group of Jews to end the deeply cherished and persistent practice of observing the Sabbath (Saturday) and instead institute a Sunday worship service? For a people steeped in tradition stretching back fifteen hundred years, this could happen only if something huge had taken place.

Bottom line: for thousands—and soon millions—of people, a massive, world-transforming, life-altering change had happened. So, what could account for it?

Many have tried to explain away the bodily resurrection of Jesus. Yet these four facts defy any other explanation but resurrection. Nothing else makes sense. At the end of the day, you can rest assured that the bodily resurrection of Jesus really happened. That fact will sustain your faith beyond any shadow of doubt.

Key Points

- Christ's resurrection is the core of Christianity.

- This is not the kind of story Christians would have invented to impress their neighbors.

- Four critical facts become unexplainable without the Resurrection.

This Week

☐ **Day 1:** Read the essay. Write the four facts on a card, and carry them with you this week.

☐ **Day 2:** Memorize 1 Corinthians 15:14.

☐ **Day 3:** Read John 11, the story of Lazarus being raised from the dead. Then read Mark 16, the story of Jesus's resurrection.

☐ **Day 4:** Meditate on Ezekiel 37:1–14 (a prediction of resurrection), John 11:25 (a promise of resurrection), and John 20:1–31 (the reality of resurrection).

☐ **Day 5:** Ask a friend what he or she thinks would happen if Abraham Lincoln rose from the dead. This question may create an opportunity for you to share your belief in Jesus's resurrection and what happened because of it.

What Do I Have to Do to Be Saved?

By grace you have been saved through faith. And this is not your own doing; it is the gift of God.

—EPHESIANS 2:8

Would you rather go to heaven or hell? Duh! Better to ask, "What do I have to do to get to heaven? What's the ticket cost?" In the big scope of things, it's hard to imagine a more important question.

Every religion has its own answer. Some require sacrifice; others, service; others, some rituals. What all have in common is that it takes human effort to get right with God. Every other religion points to something *we should do.* Christianity is *very* different. Christianity is the only religion to say we're saved not by our doing but by *what God has already done.* Salvation is God's gift offered through his sacrifice.

Grace Is God's Salvation

Paul's letter to the Romans gives us the clearest explanation of salvation by grace. Here are a few snippets: "All have sinned and fall short of the glory of God, and are justified by his grace as a gift, through the redemption that is in Christ Jesus" (3:23–24). "Since we have been justified by faith, we have peace with God through our Lord Jesus Christ. Through him we have also obtained access by faith into this grace in which we stand, and we rejoice in hope of the glory of God" (5:1–2). "Sin will have no dominion over you, since you are not under law but under grace" (6:14). "If it is by grace, it is no longer on the basis of works; otherwise grace would no longer be grace" (11:6).

Peter said the same thing: "We believe that we will be saved through the grace of the Lord Jesus, just as they will" (Acts 15:11). Jesus's half brother James agreed with Peter, stating that grace was the official stance of the church (verses 13–19).

Grace Is a Social System

In Paul's letter to the Ephesians, he went further, showing the relationship between grace, faith, and works:

> By grace you have been saved through faith. And this is not your own doing; it is the gift of God, not a result of works, so that no one may boast. For we are his workmanship, created in Christ Jesus for good works, which God prepared beforehand, that we should walk in them. (2:8–10)

These verses are both clear and confusing at the same time. We're saved by grace through faith. Yet this passage tells us that we're created for good works. So, the question is this: What's the relationship between grace, faith, and works? Put another way, if we're saved by grace, why are we expected to *do* good works? Here's the simple answer: *works are the result of our salvation, not the reason for it.* What we accomplish for Christ is a by-product of our salvation, not the foundation of it.

To understand where Paul was coming from, we need to take a trip into the first-century world. Ready? In the ancient world, about 2 percent of the population controlled virtually all the goods and services. They were called *patrons*. These patrons hired employees (or slaves) in their homes, such as doctors, lawyers, teachers, and artists. These servants were called *brokers*, and they made up approximately 5 percent of the population. Meanwhile, those employed outside the home—day laborers, farmers, craftsmen, etc.—were called *clients*. This group made up the majority of the population. This left the bottom 15 percent as "expendables" who served in the lowest occupations and had very short life spans: miners, prostitutes, ditchdiggers.

Patrons, brokers, and clients had clearly defined roles and responsibilities. The patron's job was to provide resources his clients needed to survive. Things like jobs, homes, land, medical care, and legal protection. The gifts a patron provided were called "grace."

The broker's task was to make the patron famous. How? By recruiting more clients. But wouldn't that cost the patron a lot of money? Well, of course. However, in the ancient world, honor was more valued than wealth. The more clients a patron provided for, the more honored the patron was in the community.

Finally, the clients had one primary purpose: to honor their patron. If he was running for political office, they were his biggest promoters. If he was harvesting a field, they would go work in the field. If he was addressing a crowd, they gathered to sing his praise. Don't miss this fact: while the patron would never mention his gifts again, clients were to never fail to mention as often as possible every gift they received.

There was a word the Greeks used to describe this loyalty the clients offered their patron. That word was *faith*. Perhaps a better translation is "fidelity" or "loyalty."

So, Paul's statement "By grace you have been saved through faith [fidelity]" (Ephesians 2:8) was a description of Jesus as the patron and us as his clients. Simply put, our role as Christians is to do everything we can to make Jesus famous.

Grace Is Our Service

How can we make our patron, Jesus, famous? By extending God's grace to other potential clients. Our service, then, is an act of grace. That's why our spiritual gifts are called grace: "Having gifts that differ according to the grace given to us, let us use them" (Romans 12:6). Peter said virtually the same thing: "As each has received a gift, use it to serve one another, as good stewards of God's varied grace" (1 Peter 4:10). Paul described his own ministry as an act of grace: "You have heard of the stewardship of God's grace that was given to me for you. . . . Of this gospel I was made a minister according to the gift of God's grace, which was given me by the working of his power" (Ephesians 3:2, 7).

Here's how we might summarize this process:

- God gives us grace for life and salvation.
- We give him loyalty and make Jesus famous.
- That loyalty results in service to others, which is our grace given to them.

Key Points

- Grace is what distinguishes Christianity from every other religion.

- Salvation by grace through faith directly reflects the patron-client social system of the first century.

- Our good works flow from our fidelity that we offer Jesus, our patron of grace.

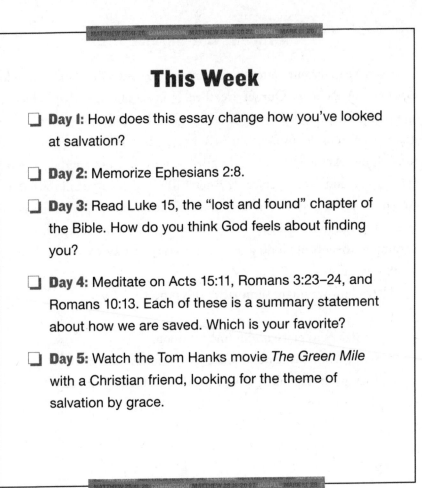

This Week

☐ **Day 1:** How does this essay change how you've looked at salvation?

☐ **Day 2:** Memorize Ephesians 2:8.

☐ **Day 3:** Read Luke 15, the "lost and found" chapter of the Bible. How do you think God feels about finding you?

☐ **Day 4:** Meditate on Acts 15:11, Romans 3:23–24, and Romans 10:13. Each of these is a summary statement about how we are saved. Which is your favorite?

☐ **Day 5:** Watch the Tom Hanks movie *The Green Mile* with a Christian friend, looking for the theme of salvation by grace.

46

Is It Possible to Have Unity in a Divided Church?

There is one body and one Spirit—just as you were called to the one hope that belongs to your call—one Lord, one faith, one baptism, one God and Father of all, who is over all and through all and in all. But grace was given to each one of us according to the measure of Christ's gift.

—EPHESIANS 4:4–7

Are you sometimes embarrassed by the church? I am. It's not so much hypocrisy that bothers me. After all, that's everywhere. What bothers me most is when we all claim Jesus as Lord but can't seem to get along. Denominations fight each other (and have even gone to war with each other). On social media, Christians attack other Christians. Why? That behavior flies in the face of Jesus's prayer the night before he died:

I do not ask for these only, but also for those who will believe in me through their word, that they may all be one, just as you, Father, are in me, and I in you, that they also may be in us, so that the world may believe that you have sent me. (John 17:20–21)

And Paul said, "There is neither Jew nor Greek, there is neither slave nor free, there is no male and female, for you are all one in Christ Jesus" (Galatians 3:28).

How can we achieve unity in the church in our own day? The answer is found in this week's core verse. Unity of the first-century church was based on each individual using his or her spiritual gift to serve the greater good.

Spiritual Gifts in the New Testament

The New Testament identifies sixteen spiritual gifts. They are listed in three passages: Romans 12:6–8; 1 Corinthians 12:4–10, 28; and Ephesians 4:7–12. Spiritual gifts are abilities given by the Holy Spirit that an individual can use to benefit the body of Christ. Some of these gifts are miraculous, such as prophecy, miracles, healing, and tongues. Most of the gifts, however, are natural abilities, such as teaching, administration, giving, and mercy.

Though some gifts may be given after salvation, most are given at birth. They're natural abilities that *become* spiritual gifts not when the Spirit gives them to us but when we give them back to God in the service of his church. Again, our abilities become gifts when we give them away, not when we receive them.

Determining and Using Your Spiritual Gift

If none of the sixteen gifts listed in the Bible fits your personal profile, don't worry! You still have a gift to offer the body of Christ. The lists of gifts in the Bible are never comprehensive. They're representative lists that paint a picture. That means there may be abilities not on the list that the Spirit has given to build up the church. For example, the first recorded spiritual gift was given to a man named Bezalel, who was tasked with building the tabernacle:

> I have called by name Bezalel the son of Uri, son of Hur, of the tribe of
> Judah, and I have filled him with the Spirit of God, with ability and
> intelligence, with knowledge and all craftsmanship, to devise artistic
> designs, to work in gold, silver, and bronze, in cutting stones for
> setting, and in carving wood, to work in every craft. (Exodus 31:2–5)

If Bezalel were alive today, he would be on Pinterest as an interior decorator. (Hey, it's a spiritual gift!)

This discussion leads to an important question: "How can I know what my spiritual gift is if it's not on the list?" This process may sound mysterious or complicated. It's not. Here is the answer in three simple steps: (1) walk into a room, (2) look around, and (3) identify what needs to be done that you would enjoy doing with excellence to benefit others. That is your spiritual gift.

Or perhaps we should clarify: that *could* be your spiritual gift . . . if you gave it back to the Holy Spirit and let him guide you in using it to serve others. Spiritual gifts are spiritual only when they benefit someone else. We never see Paul healing himself, even though he had the gift of healing. We never see generous givers using their spiritual gift to give to themselves. We don't find preachers or teachers alone in a room instructing themselves. Why? Because the purpose of every spiritual gift is to benefit others. And when we all work in that way, it promotes unity.

Spiritual gifts are to be given away. In other words, we're not buckets for God's blessings; we're pipelines. God never gives a gift to a person just because he loves that individual. This is a brilliant strategy! It makes us interdependent—we seriously need one another. It also keeps us humble since we can't do life alone. And finally, it makes us stronger together than we ever could be by ourselves.

It's our love and service that stun and attract the watching world. Go back to Jesus's prayer: "that they may all be one . . . so that the world may believe that you have sent me" (John 17:21). Gifts build unity, and unity powerfully draws outsiders into the community. Our unity is as compelling as our preaching.

In a world torn by race, class, gender, and politics, people are looking for a place to belong, a place to be accepted, and a place where it's safe to love and be loved. If you have a skill, make it spiritual by using it to serve someone in the church so someone outside the church can be drawn to Jesus.

Key Points

- Jesus's prayer in John 17 was for the unity of the church. It appears to be unanswered at this point.

- We get to answer Jesus's prayer by exercising our spiritual gifts for the benefit of the body.

- Christian unity is a powerful witness to a watching world in desperate need of belonging.

This Week

❏ **Day 1:** After reading the essay, what would you say is your spiritual gift?

❏ **Day 2:** Memorize Ephesians 4:4–7.

❏ **Day 3:** Acts 15 tells the story of the first potential split in the church. How did they resolve the conflict?

❏ **Day 4:** Based on John 17:20–21, Galatians 3:28, and Ephesians 4:11–16, what needs to happen for Christians to be unified at your school?

❏ **Day 5:** Identify something simple (1) that needs to be done, (2) that you would enjoy doing with excellence, and (3) that would help someone else. Go do that.

47

How Can Humility Help Me Succeed?

Have this mind among yourselves, which is yours in Christ Jesus, who, though he was in the form of God, did not count equality with God a thing to be grasped, but emptied himself, by taking the form of a servant, being born in the likeness of men.

—PHILIPPIANS 2:5–7

Puberty was tough on me. I was what you might call a late bloomer. I remember being paralyzed with insecurity throughout high school. *Do I belong? Am I enough? Will others like me? Can I be transparent?* I still have a bit of insecurity. I think that's why humility is difficult for me. Deep inside, I must still believe that if I don't promote myself, no one else will.

Jesus's life provides a model that sounds counterintuitive but actually works: if you humble yourself, God will exalt you.

Humility in Jesus

To say Jesus was humble hardly does him justice. He descended from heaven to earth to be born in a barn and killed on a cross. Paul used a particularly aggressive Greek word—*kenoō* ("to empty" or "to abase")—to capture the essence of Jesus's self-denial. Jesus "did not count equality with God a thing to be grasped, but emptied himself, by taking the form of a servant, being born in the likeness of men" (Philippians 2:6–7). Read that sentence again; what Paul was saying here is breathtaking.

The kind of humility Jesus showed is exactly what makes good parents, good bosses, good generals, and good coaches. It's the father on the floor wrestling with his boys. It's the boss picking up trash alongside the busboy. It's the general personally leading troops into battle. It's the coach running drills alongside her players.

None of this has to happen. Leaders can't be forced into it. Yet when it happens, followers are filled with loyalty to and respect for one who walks in their shoes.

Our modern leadership experts are finally catching up to what Jesus taught all along—the best leaders are servants of those they lead.

Humility in the Bible

All through the Bible, God commanded his people to be humble. The principle is simple and often repeated: God exalts the humble and humbles the proud.

This divine reversal is a common thread in Scripture: "Pride goes before destruction, and a haughty spirit before a fall" (Proverbs 16:18). "When they are humbled you say, 'It is because of pride'; but he saves the lowly" (Job 22:29). God turns the totem pole of human values on its head. Those on top are pushed to the bottom, and those on the bottom are lifted to the highest place.

Jesus continued this theme in his own preaching: "Whoever exalts himself will be humbled, and whoever humbles himself will be exalted"

(Matthew 23:12; see also Luke 14:11; 18:14). Both James and Peter have their own versions as well: "Humble yourselves before the Lord, and he will exalt you" (James 4:10). "Clothe yourselves, all of you, with humility toward one another, for 'God opposes the proud but gives grace to the humble.' Humble yourselves, therefore, under the mighty hand of God so that at the proper time he may exalt you" (1 Peter 5:5–6).

This leadership lesson was lost on James and John. They were audacious enough to ask for the best seats in Jesus's kingdom. Jesus rebuked them (and us): "Whoever would be first among you must be slave of all. For even the Son of Man came not to be served but to serve, and to give his life as a ransom for many" (Mark 10:44–45).

Jesus was still teaching this lesson the night before he was crucified! In the upper room, after washing their feet, Jesus again had to settle his disciples' dispute about who was the greatest: "The kings of the Gentiles exercise lordship over them, and those in authority over them are called benefactors. But not so with you. Rather, let the greatest among you become as the youngest, and the leader as one who serves" (Luke 22:25–26).

Humility in Action

We tend to think of humility as an attitude about ourselves. However, biblical humility is not so much how we feel about ourselves but how we treat others.

So, on that note, here are four suggestions for practicing humility. Don't try to be a hero and do them all right away. Set aside thirty minutes and choose one that *you can do.*

1. *Associate with the lowly as if they were celebrities.* Paul said, "Live in harmony with one another. Do not be haughty, but associate with the lowly. Never be wise in your own sight" (Romans 12:16). You could spend time with someone less popular. You could sit with an aging grandparent. You could include a person with a disability in an activity.

2. *Prioritize children.* The only time Jesus got mad at his disciples was when they tried to keep children away from him. "He was indignant and said to them, 'Let the children come to me; do not hinder them, for to such belongs the kingdom of God'" (Mark 10:14). You could volunteer with kids after school or work. Or you could babysit for free for parents who can't afford to get out otherwise.

3. *Purposely put yourself in a humble place.* In Jesus's context that meant deliberately taking a lower seat at a banquet (Luke 14:10). In our world that might mean parking farther away so others have a shorter walk. It could mean you never walk past trash without picking it up. It could look like letting someone else go ahead of you in line, emptying the dishwasher, or helping someone with homework. Whatever it looks like, it means deliberately giving up your right to privileges.

4. *Serve.* Jesus modeled service by washing his disciples' feet (John 13:1–20). Choose a task this week that you might feel is beneath you, and do it with pride.

Key Points

- Jesus's entire life—starting with his coming to earth—is a model of humility.

- The entire Bible reiterates the principle of humility—that God deposes the proud and exalts the humble.

- We can practice specific actions to grow in humility.

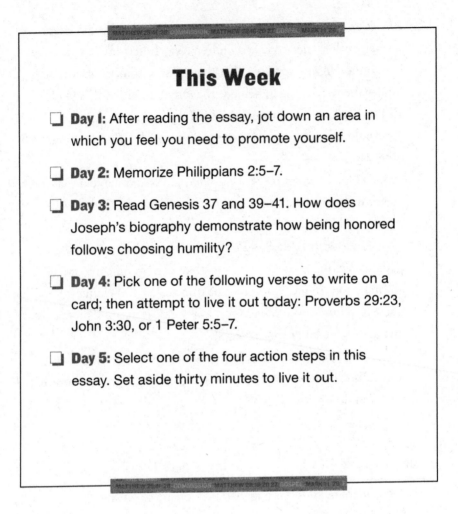

This Week

☐ **Day 1:** After reading the essay, jot down an area in which you feel you need to promote yourself.

☐ **Day 2:** Memorize Philippians 2:5–7.

☐ **Day 3:** Read Genesis 37 and 39–41. How does Joseph's biography demonstrate how being honored follows choosing humility?

☐ **Day 4:** Pick one of the following verses to write on a card; then attempt to live it out today: Proverbs 29:23, John 3:30, or 1 Peter 5:5–7.

☐ **Day 5:** Select one of the four action steps in this essay. Set aside thirty minutes to live it out.

How Can I Reduce My Anxiety?

Do not be anxious about anything, but in everything by prayer and supplication with thanksgiving let your requests be made known to God.

—PHILIPPIANS 4:6

Anxiety disorders affect forty million US adults, making them the most common mental illness in the US. And high school students often experience even more anxiety than adults. Let's get one thing clear: you're not weird or a bad person if you struggle with worry or anxiety. Homework, prom, relationships, drivers' ed, your GPA, college applications, getting a job, your parents' marriage . . . That's enough to keep anyone tied up in knots.

On the other hand, no one forces you to worry. And no one but you is fully aware of the extent of your worry. For each of us, our worry is precisely that: ours.

The good news is that worry is treatable. That's the incredible takeaway from this week's core text. Let's dig deeper. [WARNING: This essay deals with psychological and social causes of anxiety, not biochemical imbalances. If you have a medical condition, please see a qualified physician who can treat you medically.]

Worry Is Bad Theology

Worry isn't just a psychological problem; it's also a theological problem. It started in the garden when Adam and Eve decided to try to run the world on their own. Rather than living under God's authority, they declared themselves rulers of their own universe. That's exactly why you and I still worry—we try to play God, then find ourselves overwhelmed by the pressure.

Worry is toxic to our souls in two ways. It blinds us to what God *has done;* then it blocks us from what he *could do*—all because we focus on ourselves rather than God. We *so* want to do life on our own! Problem is, that disables our trust in God.

So, then, what to do? Both the Old and the New Testaments have a simple solution: trust God. This is not blind trust. It's trusting God's track record—what he has already done. He has proved himself faithful. Jesus said as much:

> Do not be anxious, saying, "What shall we eat?" or "What shall we drink?" or "What shall we wear?" For the Gentiles seek after all these things, and your heavenly Father knows that you need them all. But seek first the kingdom of God and his righteousness, and all these things will be added to you. (Matthew 6:31–33)

Look, we all know that "Do not be anxious" is easier said than done. Let's look to Jesus's teaching for a practical plan to tackle anxiety in our lives. The Gospels have more to say about eliminating worry than almost all other books of the Bible combined.

Practical Steps to Minimize Anxiety

We will never eliminate worry from our lives, but we can make great progress in decreasing it. Here is some practical advice from the Bible:

1. *Look at the world.* The first step to minimize worry is to just look around at the natural world. Jesus said, "Look at the birds of the air: they neither sow nor reap nor gather into barns, and yet your heavenly Father feeds them. Are you not of more value than they?" (Matthew 6:26). If you've ever questioned God's goodness, go outside and look around. Do the birds you see worry? In the heat of summer or the dead of winter, they always find food.

2. *Listen to God's Word.* Luke told a story about two sisters named Mary and Martha, who hosted Jesus for a meal in their home (Luke 10:38–42). Martha, the responsible older sister, dutifully prepared the bread and hummus. She wanted the meal to be perfect. After all, she was hosting the Lord of hosts. Mary, the typical younger sister, acted irresponsibly. She neglected her duties in order to sit at Jesus's feet and listen to what he said. How dare she!

   As the evening rolled on and Martha rolled her eyes with every plate she brought from the kitchen, her resentment reached a boiling point. Finally, fed up with her sister's negligence, Martha exploded to Jesus, "Tell her then to help me" (verse 40).

   One would expect Jesus to have replied by affirming a good Judeo-Christian work ethic: "Mary, do your part." Nope. He rebuked Martha instead: "Martha, Martha, you are anxious and troubled about many things, but one thing is necessary. Mary has chosen the good portion, which will not be taken away from her" (verses 41–42). When we listen to Jesus, we will have the right perspective on what's bothering us.

3. *Conquer your thoughts.* Worry is a battle of the mind. What we focus on will determine the direction our thoughts go. Neurosci-

entific research has given us the fascinating insight that protein branches hold our thoughts. In a real sense, thoughts grow like trees in our brains. The more we dwell on the thoughts, the larger the branches of proteins become.[1] We give over space and place to the thoughts we allow to dominate our minds.

This modern insight sheds light on Paul's ancient advice:

> Do not be anxious about anything, but in everything by prayer and supplication with thanksgiving let your requests be made known to God. And the peace of God, which surpasses all understanding, will guard your hearts and your minds in Christ Jesus.
>
> Finally, brothers, whatever is true, whatever is honorable, whatever is just, whatever is pure, whatever is lovely, whatever is commendable, if there is any excellence, if there is anything worthy of praise, *think about these things*. (Philippians 4:6–8)

The trick is that we can't just get rid of negative thoughts. That leaves a big hole like a vacuum, and the negativity gets sucked right back in. *The key is to replace negative thoughts with God's truth.*

Scripture, sermons, and Christian music are powerful resources for mental transformation. The thoughts we feed most will grow roots and win the battle for our brains.

Much of the time, worry is the result of feeding the wrong thoughts. Negativity is the default in our world—just look at the news and social media. As followers of Jesus, we must fight for positivity and commit to taking every thought captive for Christ (2 Corinthians 10:5).

Key Points

- Worry is negative psychology.

- Worry is bad theology.

- Jesus (along with Paul) offered insights into turning worry and anxiety to gratitude and praise.

This Week

❑ **Day 1:** Read the essay. Now jot down in the margin the top three things that bring you anxiety.

❑ **Day 2:** Memorize Philippians 4:6.

❑ **Day 3:** Read the end of Joseph's story in Genesis 42–45. Knowing the end, how would you have counseled Joseph at the beginning of his story?

❑ **Day 4:** Choose one of these verses to share with a friend who is experiencing anxiety: Matthew 6:33, Luke 10:41–42, or 2 Corinthians 10:5.

❑ **Day 5:** Carve out thirty minutes to create a list of everything you are grateful for, and post it somewhere visible: your mirror, the fridge, a school notebook, Instagram.

How Can I Find a Mentor?

What you have heard from me in the presence of many witnesses entrust to faithful men, who will be able to teach others also.

—2 Timothy 2:2

The word *mentor* never appears in the Bible. It comes from the Greek epic *The Odyssey.* (Have you had to read that in school?) Mentor was a friend of King Odysseus. When the king took off for the Trojan War, he left his son, Telemachus, and his house in Mentor's care. The goddess Athena took the form of Mentor, becoming Telemachus's teacher, counselor, and coach.[1] She was the goddess of war and wisdom. The implication is that a mentor is one who represents the divine, preparing a young person for the battles ahead.

This became true of many mentors in the Bible. Jethro mentored Moses, who had to face Pharaoh. Moses, in turn, mentored Joshua, who led the conquest of the Promised Land. Eli mentored young Samuel, who later guided Saul and David, the first kings of Israel. Elijah mentored Elisha, who confronted disobedient kings. Mordecai mentored Esther, who intervened with King Xerxes, saving her nation from extinction. Jesus mentored his twelve apostles. Barnabas mentored Paul, who paid it forward to Timothy, Titus, and many others. Mentoring was so important to Paul's ministry that in his final letter to young Timothy he pleaded with him to continue this tradition (2 Timothy 2:2).

The majority of the leaders in the Bible were mentored by someone who came before them (with a few rare exceptions like Abraham, Elijah, and Jesus). We all should take seriously our responsibility of being mentored and mentoring others.

Five Simple Steps to Find a Mentor

Even the best athletes have coaches. The better they are, the more coaches they seem to have! If we're going to be serious about making a serious impact, we would do well to get a coach. Someone who can help maximize our influence, regardless of our age or stage of life.

Many students think of a mentor as a kind of personal counselor—someone they can "do life with." Life together is great, but that's not mentoring. You do not need another sympathetic support system. What you do need is someone who can sharpen your vision, push you forward to your maximum potential, and tell you the truth even if it's uncomfortable.

Here are five steps that will help you secure a mentor:

1. *Start small and be specific.* Do not walk up to potential mentors and say, "Hey, would you mentor me?" You'll scare them off. They have no idea what kind of time or energy that requires. They'll say no before finding out. The only people you want to mentor you are people who don't have a bunch of spare time to invest in you.

   Instead, ask a potential mentor for fifteen minutes. You can meet for coffee (you buy!) or arrange a time at his or her office. Here is your request: "I've been watching you [identify a specific behavior here], and I have three coaching questions I'd like to ask, if we could schedule fifteen minutes at your convenience." This way you start out honoring the potential mentor by identifying his or her specific skills that could help you get better.

2. *Ask good questions.* Prepare your three questions beforehand. Have them written out—specific coaching questions that will allow the mentor to help you achieve a level of what he or she has achieved. (You might have your parents help you come up with some clear and insightful questions.)

   Get there early—ten to fifteen minutes before your scheduled time. Trust me, you want to be sitting there waiting on the mentor, not vice versa. Ask your three questions. Follow up each one with this question: "What is one action step I could take to carry this out?"

3. *Be respectful of the mentor's time.* At the fifteen-minute mark, thank your mentor for his or her time and excuse yourself. Even if you are invited to stay longer, respectfully decline (unless the mentor insists). Here is a great line: "I'm so grateful for your time and honored that you would extend yourself to me, but I take seriously my responsibility to respect our agreed-upon time."

4. *Follow up.* After you've completed the action steps, contact the mentor again. Ask for another fifteen minutes: "I want to thank you for those action steps you suggested. I've completed them and I've found them helpful. However, they led me to a couple more questions. Would you be willing to meet again for a follow-up?"

   After the third or fourth meeting—assuming things go well—you then could ask for a once-a-month meeting for a six-month period. If you're showing promise, few leaders could refuse to invest in a potential disciple who actually has proved to be a good investment.

5. *Have multiple mentors.* Repeat this process for three or four major areas of your life. No one person will have all the wisdom you want in every area. It's appropriate to have a mentor for school, another for sports or your job, and another for spiritual growth.

As you grow into adulthood and face things like the workforce, college, marriage, and kids, you'll want to keep expanding your network of coaches.

Key Points

- Almost every great leader of the Bible was mentored, and many in turn mentored others.

- We all need to be mentored. In fact, the more accomplished someone becomes at something, the more coaches that person tends to have.

- There are practical steps to finding a mentor. We should have multiple mentors.

This Week

☐ **Day 1:** Read the essay. Make a list of three individuals you would like to mentor you.

☐ **Day 2:** Memorize 2 Timothy 2:2.

☐ **Day 3:** Read Ruth 1–4. What practical steps did Ruth take to be mentored?

☐ **Day 4:** Meditate on Joshua 1:7, 1 Corinthians 11:1, and Philippians 4:9. What lessons do they teach about mentoring?

☐ **Day 5:** Where do you need to step it up? School? Work? Personal relationships? Your spiritual life? This week move toward getting a mentor in one of these areas by completing your list of potential mentors from Day 1 above.

50

How Do I Get Something Out of the Bible?

All Scripture is breathed out by God and profitable for teaching, for reproof, for correction, and for training in righteousness, that the man of God may be complete, equipped for every good work.

—2 Timothy 3:16–17

Reading the Bible can seem like a chore. Like taking out the trash, brushing our teeth, and unloading the dishwasher—all things we *have to do* but don't get all that excited about. But as we pointed out in the introduction, those who engage with the Bible four times a week or more also have better relationships, healthier habits, and stronger self-esteem.[1] Experience shows that reading the Bible will strengthen you in every area of your life. And like with eating food, it's important that you learn to do it for yourself.

Information < Transformation

The goal of reading the Bible is not information but transformation. You don't just want to get into the Bible; you want the Bible to get into you.

"The word of God is living and active, sharper than any two-edged sword, piercing to the division of soul and of spirit, of joints and of marrow, and discerning the thoughts and intentions of the heart" (Hebrews 4:12). God's Word has a way of penetrating our deepest secrets and greatest dreams.

With these truths in mind, a couple of simple steps will help you move from information to transformation.

1. *Pick a Bible you'll read.* There isn't one right Bible version. The right Bible for you is the one you'll read. And if you don't understand the wording, you probably won't read it! So, find a translation that's clear and motivating for you. One recommendation to consider: *The New International Version Study Bible* (NIVSB) is a great choice. It's on the pricey side, but it has a ton of helpful study tools. Here are five features the NIVSB offers that can be particularly helpful:

   • *A table of contents* lists every Bible book and the page it starts on. Each book is also divided into chapters and verses.

   • *Time lines* list Bible events in chronological order to help you see when they took place.

   • *Maps* help you find the geographic location where events took place.

   • *Introductions* to each Bible book offer a snapshot about the book's author, purpose, time, themes, and outline. Throughout each book, there are also footnotes that give brief explanations about the historical background, social values, and important words.

   • On each page are *cross-references* to several other verses that speak into the verse you are reading. (Here's how to read those references: the chapter is the number before the colon, and the verse is the number after it. So, *John 3:16* means "the book of John, chapter 3, verse 16.")

While nothing can replace an actual Bible you can hold in your hands, many people also use the free YouVersion app for reading on the run. It has many translations—even several audio versions you can listen to!

The goal is to get a Bible you *enjoy* reading and look forward to spending time with each day.

2. *Read it.* A preacher tells you to read the Bible—crazy, right? But it remains true that one of the most powerful tools God uses to encourage, challenge, and shape you is the Bible. Here are three things you need for getting the most out of your reading:

- *A place.* Choose a quiet place and a consistent time for reading your Bible. Turn your phone off and dig in. Ten to fifteen minutes is probably a good goal at first.

- *A plan.* Some people like to read straight through from Genesis to Revelation. Others want to read more chronologically, which requires jumping from book to book. The YouVersion app has a number of reading plans ranging from a single topic to the entire Bible. Perhaps the best starting place for beginners is to read from these four books: Genesis, John, Acts, and Romans. They'll provide a strong foundation for reading the whole Bible.

- *A pen.* As you read, if there's something you don't understand, jot down a question in the margin of your Bible or in a journal. Then go ask someone! Curiosity is the greatest tool for Bible study. Your pastor or study group leader can help you find answers to your questions.

  Remember that your goal is not so much information as transformation. This means your curiosity should be directed toward how you can apply these principles and teachings to your own life. You might find that writing out a prayer about the passage is a great way to grow in your

awareness of how to apply what you read. One simple plan
is to answer two questions each day:

1) What stood out to me in this passage?

2) How will I live that out practically today?

James 1:22 says it well: "Be doers of the word, and not hearers only, deceiving yourselves."

The absolute best tool for application is memorization. Identify a single verse you need to live out, and recite it aloud until you know it by heart. This approach invites the Holy Spirit to work more effectively in areas of need in your life.

Don't lose heart. Growing in the knowledge of God's Word is like any other exercise or skill: the more you do it, the more you get from it.

There'll be times when you won't feel like reading the Bible or applying it to your life. This happens to everyone. Don't be discouraged if you miss a day. Just pick up right where you left off.

"I have stored up your word in my heart, that I might not sin against you" (Psalm 119:11).

Key Points

- When you apply the Bible to your life, it brings transformation.

- A study Bible provides tools to help you get more from what you read.

- To get the most from your daily reading, you'll need a place, plan, and pen.

This Week

☐ **Day 1:** Read the essay. On a scale of 1 to 10, how are you doing with Bible reading and application?

☐ **Day 2:** Memorize 2 Timothy 3:16–17.

☐ **Day 3:** Could reading God's written Word do for you spiritually what Jesus did for people physically? He was, after all, the Word in the flesh. Read Mark 4:35–5:43 to help answer this question.

☐ **Day 4:** Meditate on Psalm 119:11, Hebrews 4:12, and James 1:22. On a scale of 1 to 10, how much value do you put on the Bible?

☐ **Day 5:** Put a check mark in each box when you accomplish the step:

☐ Purchase (or pull out) a Bible you'll read.

☐ Identify a regular place and time to read your Bible throughout the week (aim for at least four days).

☐ Choose a reading plan; it could cover anything from one book to the whole Bible.

☐ Share what your plan is with a parent or guardian.

51

How Do I Gain Grit?

Since we are surrounded by so great a cloud of witnesses, let us also lay aside every weight, and sin which clings so closely, and let us run with endurance the race that is set before us, looking to Jesus, the founder and perfecter of our faith, who for the joy that was set before him endured the cross, despising the shame, and is seated at the right hand of the throne of God.

—HEBREWS 12:1–2

Is it possible to know whether you're going to succeed in life? Well, no one can see the future, but there is a pretty good predictor. Psychologist Angela Duckworth studied thousands of individuals at the US Military Academy at West Point and at the National Spelling Bee as well as salespeople and rookie teachers in tough neighborhoods. These groups are very different, but everyone who succeeded shared one trait. Not IQ. Not wealth, race, or physical prowess.

The trait they shared was *grit*.

Grit is "passion and perseverance for long-term goals." It's the ability to stick with a difficult task not for weeks or months but for years. And it's the single most important factor in success. (Check out Dr. Duckworth's six-minute TED talk on YouTube for a great summary.)[1]

Lessons from the Hall of Fame

If grit determines success, how can we "get gritty" in our spiritual lives? Two key passages (Hebrews 11:1–12:2; Philippians 3:7–11) show us what we can learn from our heroes.

First, we look back. Who are these witnesses we read about in our core passage? They are described in a spiritual hall of fame going back through the Old Testament (Hebrews 11). Though they lived long ago, this passage pleads with us to keep them close in our minds: "All these, though commended through their faith, did not receive what was promised, since God had provided something better for us, that apart from us they should not be made perfect" (verses 39–40). Their sacrifices paved the way for us to run our own races. They're not the beer-guzzling fans in the stands. They're the weatherworn champions who finished their races and now stand beside our lanes, cheering us on. They know firsthand the sacrifice and suffering we're going through.

Ahead of everyone is Jesus Christ. His sacrifice encourages our own. Our endurance flows from his example and his presence with us.

Second, we look ahead. A reward is waiting . . . if we hold on. Our core passage states, "Let us run with endurance the race that is set before us, looking to Jesus, the founder and perfecter of our faith" (12:1–2). That's what the apostle Paul did. Look at his high-grit testimony:

Whatever gain I had, I counted as loss for the sake of Christ. Indeed, I count everything as loss because of the surpassing worth of knowing Christ Jesus my Lord. For his sake I have suffered the loss of all things and count them as rubbish, in order that I may gain Christ and be found in him, not having a righteousness of my own that comes from the law, but that which comes through faith in Christ, the righteousness from God that depends on faith—that I may know him and the power of his resurrection, and may share his sufferings, becoming like him in his death, that by any means possible I may attain the resurrection from the dead. (Philippians 3:7–11)

Five Steps for Getting Gritty

But what does grit look like on a daily basis? Although there's no magic wand to give you and me spiritual grit overnight, here are five suggestions that can help us develop it:

1. *Accept delayed gratification.* Don't trade your future for a moment! Sacrificing present pleasure for long-term gain is the starting point for any gritty person. The spiritual disciplines of fasting and prayer are practical exercises that enable this skill to spill over into all areas of life. Stick with it. The results pay off!

2. *Recognize consequences.* Every action, word, or choice has a consequence, whether good or bad. The spiritual disciplines of reading and memorizing the Bible will help you see that truth. A good starting point is the book of Proverbs. Read one chapter a day for a month. Pay attention to what it says about being wise as opposed to being a fool or a mocker. Select a verse from the chapter to memorize that will help you grow in character.

3. *Get over yourself.* The best spiritual discipline for developing this life skill is service: doing something for another who cannot pay you back. A second discipline is active listening. You could google a number of simple exercises to practice active listening. The Bible itself suggests meditation on Scripture (Psalm 1:2)—sitting quietly and envisioning a passage's implications for your life.

4. *Be accountable.* Gritty people don't do life alone. They submit their goals and habits to others who will hold them accountable. You need someone to lovingly correct you when you're wrong as well as someone to celebrate your successes. The circle you choose to surround yourself with will determine your success.

5. *Cultivate optimism.* Put simply, thank God for what you have instead of complaining about what you don't. Two super important spiritual disciplines that build optimism are worship and the Sabbath. These often work together. Worship is showing honor to

God, especially through corporate singing, communion, and preaching. Sabbath is resting from work, which rejuvenates the body, mind, and spirit. Together the two create space for optimism to flourish.

Key Points

- Grit—passion and perseverance for long-term goals—is a key to success in life.

- Grit grows when you look back at examples that came before you, as well as when you look ahead at the reward you'll reap through perseverance.

- You can take clear and practical steps to develop grit.

This Week

☐ **Day 1:** Based on this essay, would you call yourself a gritty person?

☐ **Day 2:** Memorize Hebrews 12:1–2.

☐ **Day 3:** Read Nehemiah 1–2. What did Nehemiah do to demonstrate and grow his grit?

☐ **Day 4:** Read Luke 21:19, Philippians 3:7–11, and 2 Timothy 4:7. Write each reference next to one of the five practical steps for growing grit, where you think it fits best.

☐ **Day 5:** Choose one of the steps for growing grit and follow through on it today.

What Will Heaven Be Like?

I saw a new heaven and a new earth, for the first heaven and the first earth had passed away, and the sea was no more. And I saw the holy city, new Jerusalem, coming down out of heaven from God, prepared as a bride adorned for her husband. And I heard a loud voice from the throne saying, "Behold, the dwelling place of God is with man. He will dwell with them, and they will be his people, and God himself will be with them as their God."

—REVELATION 21:1–3

The way heaven is often described in sermons, I'm not sure I want to go. Seriously, white robes, fluffy clouds, and an eternity of singing with harps? *Boring!* Fortunately, the Bible tells a different story. On a new earth with immense natural beauty, we will live in resurrected bodies but without limitations like aging, illness, and pain (1 Corinthians 15:35–49)!

What will that new earth be like? Revelation paints an incredible picture by describing what *isn't* there and what *is* there. Let's take a look.

What Isn't There

In the New Jerusalem, there will be no police, politicians, preachers, prisons, protests, doctors, lawyers, hospitals, unemployment, IRS, ICE, CIA, FBI, mothballs, locks, Kleenex, light bulbs, weddings, funerals, or armies . . . just to name a few. The last two chapters of Revelation get even more specific:

1. There'll no longer be any sea to separate peoples (21:1). Diversity will be celebrated without division, racism, or nationalism.
2. There'll be no more tears or death, no crying or pain (verse 4). No funerals, divorces, murders, thefts, gossip, broken dreams, unresolved anger, haunting memories, or lifelong regrets.
3. We won't need churches or temples because we'll continuously be in God's presence (verse 22).
4. There will be no sun or moon (verse 23). God himself will provide all the light we need!
5. There will be no curse (22:3). We won't be earning a living by the sweat of our brows. For women, there'll be no more painful childbirth. "No curse" also means there'll be no more competition, fighting, or cruelty between male and female and no more of the suffering that comes from it. God will put an end to the inequality between the sexes.
6. Nothing impure will enter the New Jerusalem (21:27). Including you and me? Yes! We'll be in heaven, but we'll no longer have any sin. That might sound too good to be true—like a fairy tale—but the impulses of our new bodies will match the intentions of our saved souls.

What Is There

Heaven will be an incredible place in light of what *isn't* there. But our hearts truly long for heaven because of what *is* there.

There'll be saints of old in heaven: Abraham, Isaac, Jacob, Peter, James, and John. Just think about the conversations we'll have!

Perhaps personally more important, our loved ones will be there. Grandparents will introduce themselves to grandchildren who knew them only through stories. Parents will see children who died in their cribs. Widows and orphans will be reunited with loved ones. Granted, the nature of the relationships will change, but how sweet it all will be!

Yet as sweet as these reunions will be, *that's not why we want to go there.*

There will also be unimaginable wealth. John described the New Jerusalem as a city of vast proportions with stunning treasure. Even the pavement is twenty-four-karat gold (Revelation 21:18–21).

The new earth will surely put this earth to shame (and God didn't do half-bad here!). No one will lack for food. Everyone will be a prince or princess in the kingdom of God.

We all dream of such luxury and comfort, *yet that's still not why we want to go to heaven.*

We'll have new bodies. No more arthritis, no more physical limitations, no more looking in the mirror and asking, "Why?" We'll have energy to work and play, and time to rest and worship.

As wonderful as it sounds, *this is not why we want to go there either.*

We want to go to heaven because Jesus is there. He's the one we've talked about, sung to, read of, and tried to follow loyally. He's waiting with outstretched arms and these words: "Well done, good and faithful servant. . . . Enter into the joy of your master" (Matthew 25:21).

I can't help but think that one glimpse of Jesus will make all our words irrelevant. He's so much grander than we've described. He's so much more glorious than we could ever imagine. We won't hug him as a buddy. We'll fall at his feet, awestruck and overwhelmed in the majesty of the moment. I imagine that it will be only his immense love that draws us back to our feet to receive his embrace.

Better Than You Imagine
and Sooner Than You Think

In the final chapter of the Bible, Jesus said three times, "I am coming soon" (Revelation 22:7, 12, 20). He is coming. There's no doubt about that. His impassioned plea to us, then, is that we come to him: "The Spirit and the Bride say, 'Come.' And let the one who hears say, 'Come.' And let the one who is thirsty come; let the one who desires take the water of life without price" (verse 17).

Here is the most amazing truth of all eternity: God loves you. In fact, he doesn't just love you; he really, really likes you. He invites you to be with him because he craves your presence (21:3).

What can we say in reply to the God of the universe, who invites us to come? The Bible actually gives us the script (22:20):

Jesus says, "Surely I am coming soon."

And we say, "Amen. Come, Lord Jesus!"

Key Points

- We're going not to heaven but to the New Jerusalem on the new earth, in physical yet glorified bodies.

- On this new earth, there will be no sickness, death, division, or decay—nothing that could bring tears to our eyes.

- The New Jerusalem will have all sorts of comfort and beauty, but we want to go there primarily because that is where Jesus is—in person and present for eternity.

This Week

❏ **Day 1:** Read the essay. What feature of heaven (other than Jesus) are you most looking forward to?

❏ **Day 2:** Memorize Revelation 21:1–3.

❏ **Day 3:** Read Revelation 21–22. What feature of the new earth (or New Jerusalem) is most surprising to you?

❏ **Day 4:** Which of these verses—John 14:2, Philippians 3:21, or Revelation 22:20—makes you most excited about the New Jerusalem?

❏ **Day 5:** Ask someone you have a relationship with whether heaven is real and what it will be like. If appropriate, ask whether that person has confidence he or she is going there.

Notes

Introduction: From Curiosity to Confidence
1. Arnold Cole and Pamela Caudill Ovwigho, *Bible Engagement as the Key to Spiritual Growth: A Research Synthesis* (Center for Bible Engagement, 2012), 4–5, https://bttbfiles.com/web/docs/cbe/Research_Synthesis _Bible_Engagement_and_Spiritual_Growth_Aug2012.pdf.

Chapter 4: How Can I Connect with God's Mission?
1. The Passover was the event in Exodus when the Israelites protected their homes from the death angel by painting their doorposts with the blood of a sacrificed lamb. On that night they were freed from slavery in Egypt.
2. Foreshadowing is a way of showing the reader what is coming in the future. Foreshadowing is commonly used in mystery movies. In the Bible, objects or events can foreshadow the saving work of Jesus.

Chapter 5: How Do I Get Right with God?
1. *Consecrate* is a religious word meaning "to make sacred" or literally "to connect to the sacred."
2. *Sanctification* means "being set apart"—that is, "the process of becoming holy." But remember, holiness begins with God declaring you to be his special possession, and only then is it followed by your behavioral transformation.

Chapter 6: Is Jesus as Good as They Say?
1. *The Transfiguration* refers to an event in Jesus's life when he was physically changed: "He was transfigured before them, and his face shone like the sun, and his clothes became white as light" (Matthew 17:2).

Chapter 7: What Is God Looking for in Leaders?

1. *The Gospels* refers to the first four books of the New Testament that chronicle Jesus's life: Matthew, Mark, Luke, and John.

Chapter 9: How Can I Find Happiness?

1. Sonja Lyubomirsky, *The How of Happiness: A Scientific Approach to Getting the Life You Want* (New York: Penguin, 2007), 20.
2. Caroline Leaf, *Switch On Your Brain: The Key to Peak Happiness, Thinking, and Health* (Grand Rapids, MI: Baker, 2015), 50, 64.

Chapter 10: Is There Proof That Jesus Is God's Son?

1. Peter W. Stoner and Robert C. Newman, *Science Speaks: Scientific Proof of the Accuracy of Prophecy and the Bible,* rev. ed. (Chicago: Moody, 1976), 101–6.
2. Stoner and Newman, *Science Speaks,* 107.

Chapter 13: If Jesus Was Rejected Back Then, Why Should I Accept Him Now?

1. "Psalm 118:22," Sefaria, www.sefaria.org/Psalms.118.22?lang=bi&with=Targum&lang2=bi, emphasis added.

Chapter 15: How Can Jesus's Death Take Care of My Problems?

1. *Atonement* means "the price paid to make something right." The Hebrew word for "atone" means "to cover."
2. "Sacrifice & Atonement," Bible Project, video, 6:50, August 27, 2015, www.youtube.com/watch?v=G_OlRWGLdnw.

Chapter 18: What Does It Take to Be #Blessed?

1. Tosefta 9:30, in *A History of the Mishnaic Law of Damages,* ed. Jacob Neusner, vol. 1, *Baba Qamma: Translation and Explanation* (Eugene, OR: Wipf and Stock, 2007), 126.
2. 4 Maccabees 10:15, in *The New Oxford Annotated Apocrypha: The Apocryphal/Deuterocanonical Books of the Old Testament,* ed. Bruce M. Metzger and Roland E. Murphy (New York: Oxford University Press,

1991), 353. The fourth book of Maccabees is a philosophical discourse using examples from around the time of the famous Maccabean revolt.

Chapter 24: Does God Want Me?

1. *Predestination* is the idea that God determines what will happen before it takes place.

Chapter 29: How Can I Find Rest?

1. *Legalism* is the idea that we gain God's approval by following rules.

Chapter 36: Can I Know I'm Saved?

1. *Eternal security* is the idea that once God saves someone, that person will always be saved, protected by God through grace.
2. *Apostasy* comes from a Greek word that literally means "to stand away from." It is the deliberate rejection of the faith and the abandonment of the Christian community.

Chapter 48: How Can I Reduce My Anxiety?

1. Caroline Leaf, *Switch On Your Brain: The Key to Peak Happiness, Thinking, and Health* (Grand Rapids, MI: Baker, 2015), 50.

Chapter 49: How Can I Find a Mentor?

1. Homer, *The Odyssey,* trans. Robert Fitzgerald (New York: Farrar, Straus and Giroux, 1998), 2.235–38, 2.282–312, 2.424–29, 3.26–33.

Chapter 50: How Do I Get Something Out of the Bible?

1. Arnold Cole and Pamela Caudill Ovwigho, *Bible Engagement as the Key to Spiritual Growth: A Research Synthesis* (Center for Bible Engagement, 2012), 4–5, https://bttbfiles.com/web/docs/cbe/Research_Synthesis _Bible_Engagement_and_Spiritual_Growth_Aug2012.pdf.

Chapter 51: How Do I Gain Grit?

1. Angela Lee Duckworth, "Grit: The Power of Passion and Perseverance," TED video, 6:01, April 2013, www.ted.com/talks/angela_lee _duckworth_grit_the_power_of_passion_and_perseverance.

About the Author

MARK E. MOORE is an acclaimed author and teaching pastor at Christ's Church of the Valley in Phoenix, Arizona. He previously spent two decades as a New Testament professor at Ozark Christian College. Mark's life passion is to make Jesus famous whether by helping people make sense of Christianity or by teaching students to understand the Bible. Mark and his wife, Barbara, reside in Phoenix.